LEVEL TWELVE

Developmental Mathematics

Solution Manual

CONCEPTS & SKILLS

12

L. George Saad, Ph. D.
Professor Emeritus
Long Island University

10 hundreds make 1 thousand

a.

1 thousand
We write: 1,000

b.

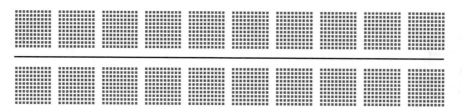

2 thousands
We write: 2,000

c.

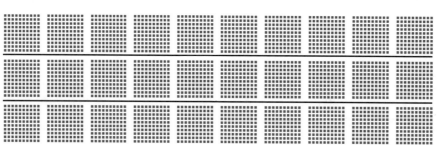

3 thousands
We write: ___3,000___

How much money is each amount?

a.	10 one-hundred dollar bills?	$1,000
b.	30 one-hundred dollar bills?	$3,000
c.	80 one-hundred dollar bills?	$8,000
d.	100 one-hundred dollar bills?	$10,000
e.	400 one-hundred dollar bills?	$40,000
f.	100 ten-dollar bills?	$1,000
g.	700 ten-dollar bills?	$7,000
h.	800 ten-dollar bills?	$8,000

APPLICATIONS

What is the number?

1. You have 8 boxes, with 1000 stamps in each box.
   How many stamps do you have? <u>8,000</u>

2. A farmer has 19 piles, with 1,000 oranges in each pile.
   How many oranges does he have? <u>19,000</u>

3. A theatre which has 1,000 seats
   was full for a whole week.
   How many persons attended? <u>7,000</u>

4. 25 students won scholarships of $1,000 each.
   How much was the total amount? <u>$25,000</u>

5. John's monthly take-home pay check is $1,000.
   How much does he receive in a year? <u>$12,000</u>

6. A restaurant serves 1,000 customers every day.
   How many customers are served during July? <u>31,000</u>

7. On the average, every day 1,000 cars go through a toll booth.
   In all, how many cars go through the booth in a year? <u>365,000</u>

8. On the average, 1,000 persons use a library every week.
   In all, how many persons use the library in a year?
   (The year is 52 weeks). <u>52,000</u>

9. A bank teller has 17 packages of money bills:
   $1,000 each
   How much money does she have? <u>$17,000</u>

10. An oil company has 28 trucks with 1000-gallon tanks.
    In all, how much oil can these trucks carry? <u>28,000 gallons</u>

Write the number:

a. What number is the same as 10 hundreds? <u>1,000</u>

b. What number is the same as 60 hundreds? <u>6,000</u>

c. What number is the same as 80 hundreds? <u>8,000</u>

d. What number is the same as 100 hundreds? <u>10,000</u>

e. What number is the same as 400 hundreds? <u>40,000</u>

f. What number is the same as 900 hundreds? <u>90,000</u>

Level 12

LARGE MONEY BILLS

- Do you know that there is a $1,000 bill? Printed on it is the portrait of Grover Cleveland, who was elected twice to the presidency: 1885-1889 and 1893-1897.

- Also, there is a $10,000 bill. Printed on it is the portrait of Salmon Chase, who was Secretary of the Treasury in President Abraham Lincoln's cabinet.

- Also, there is a $100,000 bill. Printed on it is the portrait of Woodrow Wilson, who was the president of the United States of America for two terms: 1913-1917 and 1917-1921.

APPLICATIONS

How much money is pictured in the box?

a.	b.	c.
___$3,000___	___$30,000___	___$300,000___

d.	e.	f.
___$4,000___	___$40,000___	___$400,000___

APPLICATIONS

How much money is pictured below?

a.

$241,000

b.

$320,000

c.

$103,000

How much money is each amount?

a. 9 one-hundred-thousand dollar bills. $900,000

b. 15 one-thousand dollar bills. $15,000

c. 6 ten-thousand dollar bills, and
4 one-thousand dollar bills. $64,000

d. 3 one-hundred-thousand dollar bills,
6 ten thousand-dollar bills, and
5 one-thousand-dollar bills. $365,000

e. 8 one-hundred-thousand dollar bills,
and 7 one-thousand dollar bills. $807,000

f. 9 one-hundred-thousand-dollar bills,
and 4 ten-thousand dollar bills. $940,000

g. 10 ten-thousand dollar bills. $100,000

h. 60 ten-thousand dollar bills $600,000

5

Date _____

2   ADDING

Example 1.
a. Tom has $5,000.
   Dan has $3,000 more than Tom.
   • How much does Dan have?   <u>$8,000</u>
   • How much do they have altogether?   <u>$13,000</u>

b. In a village there are 4,000 men,
   3,000 women, and 2,000 children.
   How many persons live in this village?   <u>9,000</u>

c. In a school district, there are 4,000 students
   in the elementary schools, 2,000 in
   the junior high school, and 2,000 students
   in the high school.
   How many students are in the district?   <u>8,000</u>

d. In a college, there are 5,000 women.
   There are 2,000 more men than women.
   • How many men are there?   <u>7,000</u>
   • How many students are in the college?   <u>12,000</u>

EXERCISES

Write the answer:

a.	$4,000 + 3,000 =$	<u>7,000</u>	b.	$2,000 + 7,000 =$	<u>9,000</u>
c.	$1,000 + 4,000 =$	<u>5,000</u>	d.	$5,000 + 1,000 =$	<u>6,000</u>
e.	$4,000 + 5,000 =$	<u>9,000</u>	f.	$3,000 + 2,000 =$	<u>5,000</u>
g.	$2,000 + 8,000 =$	<u>10,000</u>	h.	$9,000 + 1,000 =$	<u>10,000</u>
i.	$4,000 + 6,000 =$	<u>10,000</u>	j.	$5,000 + 5,000 =$	<u>10,000</u>
k.	$6,000 + 5,000 =$	<u>11,000</u>	l.	$9,000 + 9,000 =$	<u>18,000</u>
m.	$4,000 + 9,000 =$	<u>13,000</u>	n.	$8,000 + 7,000 =$	<u>15,000</u>
o.	$30,000 + 40,000 =$	<u>70,000</u>	p.	$50,000 + 40,000 =$	<u>90,000</u>
q.	$20,000 + 40,000 =$	<u>60,000</u>	r.	$80,000 + 20,000 =$	<u>100,000</u>
s.	$500,000 + 200,000 =$	<u>700,000</u>	t.	$300,000 + 300,000 =$	<u>600,000</u>
u.	$300,000 + 100,000 =$	<u>400,000</u>	v.	$100,000 + 600,000 =$	<u>700,000</u>

EXERCISES

Add:

a. $70,000 + 8,000 = $ __78,000__
b. $30,000 + 9,000 = $ __39,000__
c. $21,000 + 5,000 = $ __26,000__
d. $31,000 + 4,000 = $ __35,000__
e. $25,000 + 5,000 = $ __30,000__
f. $14,000 + 6,000 = $ __20,000__
g. $43,000 + 8,000 = $ __51,000__
h. $35,000 + 9,000 = $ __44,000__
i. $27,000 + 5,000 = $ __32,000__
j. $56,000 + 6,000 = $ __62,000__
k. $31,000 + 64,000 = $ __95,000__
l. $48,000 + 30,000 = $ __78,000__
m. $15,000 + 32,000 = $ __47,000__
n. $30,000 + 25,000 = $ __55,000__
o. $500,000 + 40,000 = $ __540,000__
p. $700,000 + 30,000 = $ __730,000__
q. $800,000 + 20,000 = $ __820,000__
r. $400,000 + 40,000 = $ __440,000__
s. $400,000 + 7,000 = $ __407,000__
t. $900,000 + 9,000 = $ __909,000__
u. $200,000 + 1,000 = $ __201,000__
v. $700,000 + 3,000 = $ __703,000__
w. $700,000 + 20,000 + 5,000 = $ __725,000__
x. $200,000 + 30,000 + 6,000 = $ __236,000__
y. $800,000 + 10,000 + 4,000 = $ __814,000__
z. $100,000 + 60,000 + 6,000 = $ __166,000__

APPLICATIONS

1. A family bought a house. They paid $10,000 and the bank paid $50,000. How much did the house cost?

   __$10,000 + $50,000 = $60,000__

2. The population of 3 villages is 9,000, 3,000, and 6,000. How many persons live in the 3 villages altogether?

   __9,000 + 3,000 + 6,000 = 18,000__

3. A family bought a house for $85,000. They sold the house with a profit of $7,000. For how much did they sell the house?

   __$85,000 + $ 7,000 = $92,000__

4. On Monday, a store sold goods for $15,000. The sales rose $3,000 daily for the next three days. How much were the sales on Wednesday?

   __$15,000 + $3,000 + $3,000 = $21,000__

5. There were 92,000 books in the library. 8,000 new books were added. How many books are in the library now?

   __92,000 + 8,000 = 100,000__

　　　　Level 12

Date _____

Example 2.
You want to add: 231,000 + 142,000 + 24,000
Discussion:
You may use boxes as shown to the right.
- Add the ones of thousands: 7 Th's
- Add the tens of thousands: 9 tens of Th's
- Add the hundreds of thousands: 3 hundreds of Th's

THOUSANDS		
100'S	10'S	1'S
2	3	1
1	4	2
	2	4
3	9	7

(+ on left side)

Example 3.
You want to add: 236,000 + 158,000 + 67,000
Discussion:
You may use boxes as shown to the right.
- Add the ones of thousands: 21 Th's
  21 Th's = 2 tens of Th's + 1 Th's
  Write 1 in the ones of Th's box, and
  remember that you have 2 tens of Th's
  to add to the tens of thousands.
- Add the tens of thousands: 16 tens of Th's
  16 tens of Th's = 1 hundred of Th's + 6 tens of Th's
  Write 6 in the tens of Th's box. Remember that you
  have 1 hundred of Th's to add to the hundreds of Th's.
- Add the hundreds of thousands: 4 hundreds of Th's
  Write 4 in the hundreds of thousands box.

THOUSANDS		
100'S	10'S	1'S
2	3	6
1	5	8
	6	7
4	6	1

(+ on left side)

You may, of course, do without the boxes.
Do the following additions:

a.	b.	c.	d.
232,000 41,000 + 106,000 379,000	50,000 312,000 + 127,000 489,000	291,000 38,000 + 253,000 582,000	383,000 139,000 + 49,000 571,000
e.	f.	g.	h.
139,000 378,000 + 94,000 611,000	375,000 276,000 + 24,000 675,000	789,000 81,000 + 40,000 910,000	197,000 81,000 + 342,000 620,000
i.	j.	k.	l.
48,000 118,000 + 35,000 201,000	19,000 147,000 + 238,000 404,000	39,000 251,000 + 310,000 600,000	282,000 74,000 + 144,000 500,000

APPLICATIONS

1. Last year the profits of a company were $293,000.
   This year the profits have increased by $89,000.
   How much are the profits this year?   <u>$382,000</u>

2. The population of a city is 190,000 people.
   With an increase of 26,000 per year, what
   will the population be after two years?   <u>242,000</u>

3. A company owns three canning machines. The daily
   production of the machines is 39,000 cans,
   42,000 cans, and 28,000 cans. What is the daily
   production of the three machines altogether?   <u>109,000 cans</u>

4. A textile firm produced three kinds of fabric:
       1st kind: 39,000 yards
       2nd kind: 84,000 yards
       3rd kind: 77,000 yards
   How many yards did the company
   produce of the three kinds?   <u>200,000</u>

5. A publishing company published a certain book
   three times:
       1st time: 75,000 copies
       2nd time: 87,000 copies
       3rd time: 115,000 copies
   How many copies of this book were published?   <u>277,000</u>

6. A, B, and C are three numbers.
   A is 36,000, B is 19,000 more than A,
   and C is 28,000 more than B.
   What number is B?   <u>$B = 36,000 + 19,000 = 55,000$</u>
   What number is C?   <u>$C = 55,000 + 28,000 = 83,000$</u>

7. $M = 39,000$
   $N = M + 81,000$
   $X = N + 25,000$
   What number is N?   <u>$N = 39,000 + 81,000 = 120,000$</u>
   What number is X?   <u>$X = 120,000 + 25,000 = 145,000$</u>

3 SUBTRACTING

Example 1.

Last year, Ted's income was $9,000. He spent $7,000.
How much did he save?

Solution:

9 Th's - 7 Th's = 2 Th's

So, 9,000 - 7,000 = 2,000   Ted saved $2,000.

$$\begin{array}{r} 9,000 \\ -\ 7,000 \\ \hline 2,000 \end{array}$$

Example 2.

The population of a village is 14,000. 8,000 are males.
How many females live in the village?

Solution:

The number of females = 14,000 - 8,000 = 6,000

$$\begin{array}{r} 14,000 \\ -\ 8,000 \\ \hline 6,000 \end{array}$$

Example 3.

During January 1999, a bus line carries 700,000 passengers.
During February 1999, the number of passengers decreased by 200,000.
How many passengers used the bus line during February 1999?

Solution:

700, 000 - 200,000 = 500,000

During February 1984, 500,000 passengers used the bus line.

EXERCISES

Write the answer:

1. a. 9,000 - 4,000 = _5,000_   b. 8,000 - 2,000 = _6,000_
    c. 7,000 - 3,000 = _4,000_   d. 6,000 - 6,000 = _0_

2. a. 11,000 - 2,000 = _9,000_   b. 14,000 - 5,000 = _9,000_
    c. 12,000 - 7,000 = _5,000_   d. 17,000 - 9,000 = _8,000_
    e. 10,000 - 4,000 = _6,000_   f. 10,000 - 1,000 = _9,000_

3. a. 90,000 - 70,000 = _20,000_   b. 40,000 - 30,000 = _10,000_
    c. 60,000 - 40,000 = _20,000_   d. 80,000 - 80,000 = _0_

4. a. 37,000 - 5,000 = _32,000_   b. 86,000 - 6,000 = _80,000_
    c. 950,000 - 30,000 = _920,000_ d. 840,000 - 40,000 = _800,000_

5. a. 40,000 - 7,000 = _33,000_   b. 90,000 - 6,000 = _84,000_
    c. 31,000 - 4,000 = _27,000_   d. 56,000 - 9,000 = _47,000_

Example 4.
You want to subtract: 978,000 - 246,000
Discussion:
You may use boxes.

	THOUSANDS		
	100'S	10'S	1'S
	9	7	8
-	2	4	6
	7	3	2

- 8 Th's - 6 Th's = 2 Th's
- 7 tens of Th's - 4 tens of Th's = 3 tens of Th's
- 9 hundreds of Th's - 2 hundreds of TH's = __7 hundreds of Th's__

The answer is __732,000__

Example 5.
Do the subtraction to the right.

	THOUSANDS		
	100'S	10'S	1'S
	6	5	1
-	2	8	7
	3	6	4

Solution:
- 11 Th's - 7 Th's = 4 Th's
- 14 tens of Th's - 8 tens of Th's = 6 tens of Th's
- 5 hundreds of Th's - 2 hundreds of Th's = __3 hundreds of Th's__

The answer is __364,000__

Example 6.
Do the subtraction to the right.

	THOUSANDS		
	100'S	10'S	1'S
	7	2	3
-	1	9	8
	5	2	5

Solution:
- 13 Th's - 8 Th's = 5 Th
- 11 tens of Th's - 9 tens of Th's = 2 tens of Th's
- 6 hundreds of Th's - 1 hundred of Th's = __5 hundreds of Th's__

The answer is __525,000__

You may, of course, do without the boxes.
Do the following subtractions:

a.	b.	c.	d.
642,000 - 118,000 524,000	913,000 - 851,000 62,000	835,000 - 149,000 686,000	740,000 - 395,000 345,000
e.	f.	g.	h.
810,000 - 283,000 527,000	805,000 - 463,000 342,000	901,000 - 265,000 636,000	800,000 - 365,000 435,000
i.	j.	k.	l.
834,000 - 96,000 738,000	470,000 - 84,000 386,000	700,000 - 98,000 602,000	107,000 - 88,000 19,000

EXERCISES

Subtract:

1. a. 9,000 - 4,000 = __5,000__ b. 14,000 - 5,000 = __9,000__

   c. 8,000 - 1,000 = __7,000__ d. 12,000 - 7,000 = __5,000__

   e. 90,000 - 80,000 = __10,000__ f. 800,000 - 300,000 = __500,000__

   g. 40,000 - 30,000 = __10,000__ h. 900,000 - 500,000 = __400,000__

   i. 25,000 - 5,000 = __20,000__ j. 85,000 - 3,000 = __82,000__

   k. 48,000 - 8,000 = __40,000__ l. 46,000 - 5,000 = __41,000__

   m. 930,000 - 30,000 = __900,000__ n. 740,000 - 30,000 = __710,000__

   o. 750,000 - 50,000 = __700,000__ p. 680,000 - 50,000 = __630,000__

   q. 49,000 - 23,000 = __26,000__ r. 78,000 - 28,000 = __50,000__

   s. 85,000 - 31,000 = __54,000__ t. 69,000 - 39,000 = __30,000__

2.

a.	b.	c.	d.
798,000 - 261,000 537,000	685,000 - 243,000 442,000	291,000 - 38,000 253,000	465,000 - 217,000 248,000
e.	f.	g.	h.
715,000 - 496,000 219,000	823,000 - 165,000 658,000	760,000 - 194,000 566,000	640,000 - 295,000 345,000
i.	j.	k.	l.
610,000 - 441,000 169,000	910,000 - 284,000 626,000	703,000 - 151,000 552,000	302,000 - 92,000 210,000
m.	n.	o.	p.
801,000 - 148,000 653,000	603,000 - 298,000 305,000	700,000 - 125,000 575,000	800,000 - 194,000 606,000

1. Carol is a real estate saleswoman.
   She sold two houses for $150,000.
   One of the house was sold for $60,000.
   How much was the price of the second house?

   $150,000 - $60,000 = $90,000

2. The number of books in a library
   increased from 197,000 to 203,000.
   How many books were added?

   203,000 - 197,000 = 6,000

3. The population of a village is 14,000.
   5,000 are men and 6,000 are women.
   How many children are there?

   a. 5,000 + 6,000 = 11,000
   b. 14,000 - 11,000 = 3,000

4. Every year John gets an increase of $3,000.
   This year his salary is $25,000.
   a. What was his salary last year?
   b. What will his salary be next year?

   a. $25,000 - $3,000 = $22,000
   b. $25,000 + $3,000 = $28,000

5. In three years the profits of a company
   totaled $915,000. The profits in the first
   year were $276,000 and in the second
   year were $385,000.
   What were the profits in the third year?

   a. $276,000 + $385,000 = $661,000
   b. $915,000 - $661,000 = $254,000

6. You started with a number, added 30,000,
   and then subtracted 90,000.
   The answer was 10,000.
   What was the number?

   a. 10,000 + 90,000 = 100,000
   b. 100,000 - 30,000 = 70,000

7. A, B, and C are three numbers.
   A is 192,000, B is 89,000 more than A,
   and C is 65,000 less than B.
   What number is C?

   a. B = 192,000 + 89,000 = 281,000
   b. C = 281,000 - 65,000 = 216,000

8. You subtracted a number from 795,000
   and added 134,000.
   The answer was 600,000.
   What was the number?

   a. 600,000 - 134,000 = 466,000
   b. 795,000 - 466,000 = 329,000

9. The difference between two numbers is 20,000.
   The smaller number is 170,000.
   Find the other number.

   170,000 + 20,000 = 190,000

13

4   MULTIPLYING

Example 1:
   There are 1,000 stamps in each envelope.
   In all, how many stamps are there?

Discussion:
- There are 3 rows of envelopes.
- In each row, there are 4 envelopes.
- In all, there are 3 x 4 = 12 envelopes.
- In all, there are 3 x 4,000 = 12,000 stamps.

Similarly:

a. 8 x 7,000 = _56,000_	b. 9 x 6,000 = _54,000_
c. 2 x 5,000 = _10,000_	d. 5 x 8,000 = _40,000_
e. 9 x 9,000 = _81,000_	f. 4 x 5,000 = _20,000_
g. 7 x 6,000 = _42,000_	h. 5 x 6,000 = _30,000_

Example 2:
   Suppose you have 7 very long strings of beads with 3,000 in each string.
   A part of the arrangement is shown below.
   In all, how many beads are there?

- You may see the beads as 7 sets with 3,000 beads in each set.
  In all, there are 7 x 3,000 = 21,000 beads.
- You also may see the beads as 3,000 sets with 7 beads in each set.
  In all, there are 3,000 x 7 = 21,000 beads.

Similarly:

a. 3 x 9,000 = _27,000_ 9,000 x 3 = _27,000_	b. 4 x 6,000 = _24,000_ 6,000 x 4 = _24,000_
c. 6 x 8,000 = _48,000_ 8,000 x 6 = _48,000_	d. 7,000 x 3 = _21,000_ 3 x 7,000 = _21,000_
e. 5 x 8,000 = _40,000_ 8,000 x 5 = _40,000_	f. 8,000 x 8 = _64,000_ 8 x 8,000 = _64,000_

EXERCISES

Write the answer:

1. a. $3 \times 6,000 =$ ___18,000___   b. $7 \times 4,000 =$ ___28,000___
    c. $6 \times 2,000 =$ ___12,000___   d. $6 \times 5,000 =$ ___30,000___
    e. $9 \times 8,000 =$ ___72,000___   f. $6 \times 7,000 =$ ___42,000___

2. a. $4,000 \times 5 =$ ___20,000___   b. $5,000 \times 4 =$ ___20,000___
    c. $7,000 \times 8 =$ ___56,000___   d. $9,000 \times 6 =$ ___54,000___
    e. $6,000 \times 7 =$ ___42,000___   f. $8,000 \times 5 =$ ___40,000___

3. a. $5 \times 102,000 =$ ___510,000___   b. $3 \times 294,000 =$ ___882,000___
    c. $9 \times 104,000 =$ ___936,000___   d. $4 \times 208,000 =$ ___832,000___
    e. $4 \times 236,000 =$ ___944,000___   f. $8 \times 89,000 =$ ___712,000___

4. a. $324,000 \times 3 =$ ___972,000___   b. $164,000 \times 5 =$ ___820,000___
    c. $125,000 \times 6 =$ ___750,000___   d. $208,000 \times 4 =$ ___832,000___
    e. $79,000 \times 9 =$ ___711,000___   f. $85,000 \times 8 =$ ___680,000___

APPLICATIONS

1. A canning plant produces 185,000 cans a day. How many cans are produced in the 5 working days of the week?

    $5 \times 185,000 = 925,000$

2. A textile factory produced 74,000 yards of material. They were sold for $3 a yard. For how much were they sold?

    $74,000 \times \$3 = \$222,000$

3. A jet airliner covered six 5,000-mile trips and eight 4,000-mile trips. Altogether, how many miles did the jet cover?

    a. $6 \times 5,000 = 30,000$
    b. $8 \times 4,000 = 32,000$
    c. Altogether: 62,000

4. $M = 4,000$
    $N =$ twice M
    $P = 9$ times N.
    What number is P?

    $N = 2 \times 4,000 = 8,000$
    $P = 9 \times 8,000 = 72,000$

5. A is 85,000, B is 79,000 more than A, and C is 3 times B. What number is C?

    $B = 164,000$
    $C = 3 \times 164,000 = 492,000$

Example 3.

A garment factory produces 23,000 suits each month.
How many suits are produced in a year?

$$\begin{array}{r} 23 \\ \times\ 12 \\ \hline 46 \\ 23 \\ \hline 276 \end{array}$$

Discussion:

- The situation calls for the multiplication: 12 x 23,000.
- The answer to (12 x 23,000) is the same as
  (12 x 23) in thousands.
  12 x 23 = 276
  12 x 23,000 = 276,000

Example 4.

Find the answer: 29 x 32,000

$$\begin{array}{r} 29 \\ \times\ 32 \\ \hline 58 \\ 87 \\ \hline 928 \end{array}$$

a. 29 x 32 = __928__

b. 29 x 32,000 = __928,000__

Example 5.

Find the answer: 25,000 x 38

$$\begin{array}{r} 25 \\ \times\ 38 \\ \hline 200 \\ 75 \\ \hline 950 \end{array}$$

a. 25 x 38 = __950__

b. 25,000 x 38 = __950,000__

EXERCISES

Multiply:

a. 23 x 25,000	b. 35 x 12,000	c. 43,000 x 18
__575,000__	__420,000__	__774,000__
d. 26,000 x 32	e. 17,000 x 29	f. 36 x 25,000
__832,000__	__493,000__	__900,000__

APPLICATIONS

1. One week, a poultry farm produced
   18,000 dozens of eggs.
   How many eggs were produced that week?

   $\underline{18,000 \times 12 = 216,000}$

2. The monthly expenses of a company
   is $38,000.
   How much are the yearly expenses?

   $\underline{12 \times \$38,000 = \$456,000}$

3. The textile factory produces 14,000
   yards of curtain material each week.
   How many yards of material are produced
   in one year?

   $\underline{52 \times 14,000 = 728,000}$

4. A builder built 25 houses, with
   the cost of $39,000 per house.
   How much did the project cost?

   $\underline{25 \times \$39,000 = 975,000}$

5. Find the answer:
   a. $(24 \times 32,000) - 76,000$ b. $(41,000 \times 16) + 25,000$

   $\underline{768,000 - 76,000 = 692,000}$ $\underline{656,000 + 25,000 = 681,000}$

6. Find the sum of $(28 \times 24,000)$
   and $(17,000 \times 15)$

   $\underline{672,000 + 255,000 = 927,000}$

7. Find the difference between
   $(16,000 \times 28)$ and $(39,000 \times 14)$

   $\underline{546,000 - 448,000 = 98,000}$

Date_____

5 DIVIDING

Example 1.

You have 2,000 items. Below is a picture of a part of the arrangement.

Discussion:

a. You may see the arrangement as 2 equivalent sets.
The following equation applies: $2,000 \div 2 = 1,000$
Result: 1,000 items in each set.

b. You also may see the arrangement as 2 equivalent sets.
The following equation applies: $2,000 \div 2 = 1,000$
Result: 1,000 sets are made.

Note:

In both cases, the equation "$2,000 \div 2 = 1,000$" applies, but in a, the answer is "1,000 items in each set", and, in b, the answer is "1,000 sets are made".

Example 2.

You have 8,000 stamps. Below is a picture of a part of the arrangement.

Discussion:

a. Divide them equally into 4 sets.
 • You have 8 identical rows.
 • You divide them equally into 4 sets.
  $8 \div 4 = 2$ 2 rows in each set
  $8,000 \div 4 = 2,000$ 2,000 stamps in each set.

b. Make them into sets with 4 stamps in each set.
 • Looking vertically, you see that there are 1,000 groups, 8 stamps each.
 • Each of these groups may be made into 2 fours.
  1,000 groups make 2,000 fours.
 • $8,000 \div 4 = 2,000$ 2,000 sets are made.

Note:

In both cases, the equation "$8,000 \div 4 = 2,000$" applies, but in example a, the answer is "2,000 items in each set" and, in example b, the answer is "2,000 sets are made."

APPLICATIONS

What does the answer tell?

1. a. A stationery store received 24,000
       pens in 4 boxes, with the same
       number of pens in each box.
                    $24,000 \div 4 = 6,000$ 6,000 pens in each box

    b. A stationery store received 24,000
       pens in packs, 4 pens each.
                    $24,000 \div 4 = 6,000$ 6,000 packs were received

2. a. A bank teller has $40,000 in five-
       dollar bills.
                    $\$40,000 \div \$5 = 8,000$ 8,000 bills

    b. A bank teller has $40,000 in 5 packs,
       with the same amount in each pack.
                    $\$40,000 \div 5 = \$8,000$ $8,000 in each pack

3. An auto factory charged a dealer $21,000
    for 3 identical cars.
                    $\$21,000 \div 3 = \$7,000$ $7,000 paid for each car

4. A supermarket collected $60,000 selling
    cookies at $2 a pound.
                    $\$60,000 \div \$2 = 30,000$ 30,000 pounds were sold

5. A soda factory produced 400,000 cans in
    8-can packs.
                    $400,000 \div 8 = 50,000$ 50,000 packs were produced

EXERCISES

Write the answer:

$42,000 \div 7 =$	6,000	$24,000 \div 4 =$	6,000	$12,000 \div 6 =$	2,000
$35,000 \div 5 =$	7,000	$12,000 \div 3 =$	4,000	$14,000 \div 7 =$	2,000
$32,000 \div 8 =$	4,000	$18,000 \div 6 =$	3,000	$8,000 \div 2 =$	4,000
$6,000 \div 6 =$	1,000	$54,000 \div 9 =$	6,000	$24,000 \div 8 =$	3,000
$16,000 \div 2 =$	8,000	$21,000 \div 7 =$	3,000	$4,000 \div 4 =$	1,000
$8,000 \div 8 =$	1,000	$25,000 \div 5 =$	5,000	$28,000 \div 7 =$	4,000
$18,000 \div 9 =$	2,000	$36,000 \div 4 =$	9,000	$16,000 \div 8 =$	2,000
$10,000 \div 5 =$	2,000	$14,000 \div 2 =$	7,000	$27,000 \div 3 =$	9,000
$49,000 \div 7 =$	7,000	$15,000 \div 3 =$	5,000	$54,000 \div 6 =$	9,000

Example 3.
   Do the division to the right.
Dicussion:

$$\frac{234{,}000}{2)468{,}000}$$

   The number is made of
   4 hundreds of thousands,
   6 tens of thousands, and
   8 thousands.
   You divide in three steps:
   - 4H's of Th's ÷ 2 = 2H's of Th's
   - 6T's of Th's ÷ 2 = 3T's of Th's
   - 8 Th's ÷ 2 = 4Th's

The answer is 234 Th's which is written ___234,000___

Example 4.
   Do the division to the right.
Discussion:

$$\frac{079{,}000}{5)395{,}000}$$

   The dividend is composed of: 3H's of Th's,
   9T's of Th's, and 5 Th's
   You divide step by step.
   - 3H's of Th's ÷ 5 = 0H's of Th's and 3H's of Th's remain.
   - 39 T's of Th's ÷ 5 = 7T's of Th's and 4 T's of Th's remain.
   - 45 Th's ÷ 5 = 9Th's.

The answer is 079 Th's which is written ___79,000___

Example 5.
   You multiplied a number by 25.
   The answer was 675,000.
   What was the number?
Discussion:

$$\begin{array}{r} 027 \\ 25)\overline{675} \\ \underline{50} \\ 175 \\ \underline{175} \end{array} \qquad \begin{array}{r} 027{,}000 \\ 25)\overline{675{,}000} \\ \underline{50} \\ 175 \\ \underline{175} \end{array}$$

   - The situation calls for the division: 675,000 ÷ 25.
   - 675,000 is the same as 675 thousands.
     675 Th's ÷ 25 = 27 Th's
   - So, 675,000 ÷ 25 = 27,000

Example 6.
   Do the division:

$$\begin{array}{r} 015{,}000 \\ 38)\overline{570{,}000} \\ \underline{38} \\ 190 \\ \underline{190} \end{array}$$

Example 7.
   Do the division:

$$\begin{array}{r} 006{,}000 \\ 125)\overline{750{,}000} \\ \underline{750} \end{array}$$

EXERCISES

1.

a. $\dfrac{111,000}{5)555,000}$	b. $\dfrac{210,000}{3)630,000}$	c. $\dfrac{211,000}{4)844,000}$	d. $\dfrac{342,000}{2)684,000}$
e. $\dfrac{320,000}{3)960,000}$	f. $\dfrac{120,000}{4)480,000}$	g. $\dfrac{401,000}{2)802,000}$	h. $\dfrac{102,000}{3)306,000}$
i. $\dfrac{181,000}{4)724,000}$	j. $\dfrac{131,000}{5)655,000}$	k. $\dfrac{141,000}{7)987,000}$	l. $\dfrac{081,000}{8)648,000}$
m. $\dfrac{219,000}{4)876,000}$	n. $\dfrac{319,000}{3)957,000}$	o. $\dfrac{349,000}{2)698,000}$	p. $\dfrac{112,000}{8)896,000}$
q. $\dfrac{144,000}{3)432,000}$	r. $\dfrac{234,000}{4)936,000}$	s. $\dfrac{079,000}{5)395,000}$	t. $\dfrac{125,000}{7)875,000}$
u. $\dfrac{407,000}{2)814,000}$	v. $\dfrac{305,000}{3)915,000}$	w. $\dfrac{206,000}{4)824,000}$	x. $\dfrac{103,000}{7)721,000}$

2.

a. $\begin{array}{r}019,000\\15)\overline{285,000}\\\underline{15}\\135\\\underline{135}\end{array}$	b. $\begin{array}{r}031,000\\25)\overline{775,000}\\\underline{75}\\25\\\underline{25}\end{array}$	c. $\begin{array}{r}036,000\\18)\overline{648,000}\\\underline{54}\\108\\\underline{108}\end{array}$	d. $\begin{array}{r}034,000\\24)\overline{816,000}\\\underline{72}\\96\\\underline{96}\end{array}$
e. $\begin{array}{r}025,000\\34)\overline{850,000}\\\underline{68}\\170\\\underline{170}\end{array}$	f. $\begin{array}{r}030,000\\24)\overline{720,000}\\\underline{72}\end{array}$	g. $\begin{array}{r}024,000\\35)\overline{840,000}\\\underline{70}\\140\\\underline{140}\end{array}$	h. $\begin{array}{r}015,000\\46)\overline{690,000}\\\underline{46}\\230\\\underline{230}\end{array}$
i. $\begin{array}{r}028,000\\25)\overline{700,000}\\\underline{50}\\200\\\underline{200}\end{array}$	j $\begin{array}{r}025,000\\32)\overline{800,000}\\\underline{64}\\160\\\underline{160}\end{array}$	k. $\begin{array}{r}025,000\\24)\overline{600,000}\\\underline{48}\\120\\\underline{120}\end{array}$	l. $\begin{array}{r}004,000\\125)\overline{500,000}\\\underline{500}\end{array}$

Level 12

APPLICATIONS

1. A stationery store received two shipments of
   pens: 9 boxes with 3,000 pens in each box,
   and 5,000 packs with 3 pens in each pack.
   In all, how many pens were received?

   a. 9 x 3,000 = 27,000
   b. 5,000 x 3 = 15,000
   c. In all: 42,000

2. Sue, a bank teller, has 2,000 five-dollar
   bills and 1,000 ten dollar bills.
   How much money does she have?

   a. 2,000 x $5 = $10,000
   b. 1,000 x $10 = $10,000
   c. In all: $20,000

3. A department store received 2,000
   boxes with 3 shirts in each box.
   All shirts were sold for $5 each.
   How much money was the total sale?

   a. 2,000 x 3 = 6,000
   b. 6,000 x $5 = $30,000

4. During the last six months, a jet liner covered
   186,000 miles. Assuming that it flies the same
   trips each month,
   a. How many miles does it cover each month?
   b. How many miles does it cover in 5 months?

   186,000 ÷ 6 = 031,000
   5 x 31,000 = 155,000

5. In the supply room there are 12,000 pencils
   in 6-pencil packs, and 12,000 erasers in
   4-eraser packs.
   How many packs are there?

   a. 12,000 ÷ 6 = 2,000
   b. 12,000 ÷ 4 = 3,000
   c. In all: 5,000

6. A bank teller has $31,000.
   She has 10 one-hundred-dollar bills, and
   the rest in five-dollar bills.
   How many five-dollar bills does she have?

   a. 10 x $100 = $1,000
   b. $31,000 - $1,000 = $30,000
   c. $30,000 ÷ 5 = $6,000

7. Find the number which is 39,000 less than 8 times 63,000.

    a. 8 x 63,000 = 504,000
    b. 504,000 - 39,000 = 465,000

8. Find the number which is 4 times the sum of 29,000 and 148,000.

    a. 29,000 + 148,000 = 177,000
    b. 4 x 177,000 = 708,000

9. You multiplied a number by 8 and then added 18,000. The answer was 418,000.
    What was the number?

    a. 418,000 - 18,000 = 400,000
    b. 400,000 ÷ 8 = 50,000

10. You multiplied a number by 6 and then divided by 5. The answer was 36,000.
    What was the number?

    a. 36,000 x 5 = 180,000
    b. 180,000 ÷ 6 = 30,000

11. A = 38,000
    B = 4 x A
    C = A + B
    What number is C?

    B = 4 x 38,000 = 152,000
    C = 38,000 + 152,000 = 190,000

12. M = 214,000
    N = 3 x M - 78,000
    What number is N?

    a. 3 x 214,000 = 642,000
    b. 642,000 - 78,000 = 564,000

Date_____

UNIT A TEST

1. How much money is pictured below?

a.
$4,000

b.
$20,000

c.
$300,000

d.
$213,000

e.
$301,000

2. Write the answer:

a. 4,000 + 2,000 = __6,000__   b. 3,000 + 6,000 = __9,000__
c. 2,000 + 8,000 = __10,000__   d. 9,000 + 1,000 = __10,000__
e. 8,000 + 6,000 = __14,000__   f. 7,000 + 5,000 = __12,000__

3. Add:

a.
```
   521,000
    34,000
 + 142,000
   697,000
```
b.
```
   496,000
    87,000
 + 164,000
   747,000
```
c.
```
   269,000
   132,000
 +  69,000
   470,000
```
d.
```
    79,000
   648,000
 + 173,000
   900,000
```

4. Write the answer:

a. 7,000 - 6,000 = __1,000__   b. 9,000 - 7,000 = __2,000__
c. 10,000 - 4,000 = __6,000__   d. 10,000 - 3,000 = __7,000__
e. 11,000 - 8,000 = __3,000__   f. 14,000 - 8,000 = __6,000__

5. Subtract:

a.
```
   968,000
 - 427,000
   541,000
```
b.
```
   547,000
 - 489,000
   058,000
```
c.
```
   840,000
 - 276,000
   564,000
```
d.
```
   900,000
 - 148,000
   752,000
```

6. Write the answer:
   a. 5 x 7,000 = __35,000__
   c. 6,000 x 5 = __30,000__
   b. 9 x 6,000 = __54,000__
   d. 8,000 x 9 = __72,000__

7. Multiply:
   a. 8 x 79,000
   b. 36 x 19,000
   c. 25,000 x 24

   = 632,000
   = 684,000
   = 600,000

8. Write the answer:
   a. 45,000 ÷ 5 = __9,000__
   c. 56,000 ÷ 7 = __8,000__
   e. 72,000 ÷ 9 = __8,000__
   b. 20,000 ÷ 4 = __5,000__
   d. 49,000 ÷ 7 = __7,000__
   f. 27,000 ÷ 3 = __9,000__

9. Divide:

   a. $\frac{121,000}{4)484,000}$

   b. $\frac{047,000}{5)235,000}$

   c. $\frac{025,000}{8)200,000}$

   d. $\frac{009,000}{15)135,000}$
   135

   e. $\frac{015,000}{26)390,000}$
   26
   130
   130

   f. $\frac{008,000}{123)984,000}$
   984

10. A builder built 9 houses: 5 for $75,000 each and 4 for $69,000 each. How much did the project cost?

    a. 5 x $75,000 = $375,000
    b. 4 x $69,000 = $276,000
    c. Total Cost $651,000

11. A bank branch started with 4,000 five-dollar bills. During the day, $19,000 was deposited, and $28,000 was withdrawn by customers. How much money was in the bank at the end of the day?

    a. 4,000 x $5 = $20,000
    b. $20,000 + $19,000 = $39,000
    c. $39,000 - $28,000 = $11,000

12. Divide the sum of 49,000 and 131,000 by 12.

    a. 49,000 + 131,000 = 180,000
    b. 180,000 ÷ 12 = 15,000

13. You started with 35,000. You subtracted a number and then multiplied by 7. The answer was 168,000. What was the number?

    a. 168,000 ÷ 7 = 24,000
    b. 35,000 - 24,000 = 11,000

14. A = 3 x 7,000
    B = A + 9,000
    C = B - 5,000
    What number is C?

    A = 21,000
    B = 21,000 + 9,000 = 30,000
    C = 30,000 - 5,000 = 25,000

Date _____

How many dollars are pictured below?

- You may use boxes as shown to the right.
- The number presented is written 3,142 or 3142.
- It is read: three thousand one hundred forty-two

1,000'S	100'S	10'S	1'S
3	1	4	2

How many dollars are pictured below?

- Fill in the boxes.
- How is the numeral written? **2,030 or 2030.**
- How is the number read?   **two thousand thirty**

1,000'S	100'S	10'S	1'S
2	0	3	0

How many dollars are pictured below?

- Fill in the boxes.
- How is the numeral written? **1,032 or 1032.**
- How is the numeral read?   **one thousand thirty-two**

1,000'S	100'S	10'S	1'S
1	0	3	2

How many dollars are pictured below?

- Fill in the boxes.
- How is the numeral written? **2,003 or 2003.**
- How is the numeral read?   **two thousand three**

1,000'S	100'S	10'S	1'S
2	0	0	3

APPLICATIONS

1. How many dollars are pictured?

a.

$2,100

b.

$3,020

c.

$1,002

2. In the numeral to the right: **3,972**
   a. The 2 represents the number of ___ones___
   b. The 7 represents the number of ___tens___
   c. The 9 represents the number of ___hundreds___
   d. The 3 represents the number of ___thousands___

3. Write a numeral for:
   a. 8 thousands, 9 hundreds, 6 tens, and 7 ones. ___8967___
   b. 7 thousands, 5 tens, and 6 ones. ___7056___
   c. 3 thousands, 2 tens, and 9 ones. ___3029___
   d. 8 thousands and 4 tens. ___8040___
   e. 3 tens and 9 hundreds. ___930___
   f. 4 thousands and 3 ones. ___4003___

4. Write a numeral for:
   a. 7,000 + 500 + 30 + 9 ___7539___
   b. 8,000 + 40 ___8040___
   c. 9,000 + 8 ___9008___
   d. 4,000 + 600 ___4600___
   e. 1,000 + 30 + 7 ___1037___
   f. 2,000 + 400 + 8 ___2408___

B

Level 12

7   ADDING

Example 1.

You want to add: 3014 + 2341 + 4323

Discussion:

You may also use boxes as shown to the right.

1,000'S	100'S	10'S	1'S
3	0	1	4
2	3	4	1
+ 4	3	2	3
9	6	7	8

- Add ones: 8 ones
- Add tens: 7 tens
- Add hundreds: 6 hundreds
- Add thousands: 9 thousands

The answer is ___9,678___

Example 2.

You want to do the addition to the right.

Discussion:

1,000'S	100'S	10'S	1'S
3	5	6	7
	1	8	6
+ 2	5	2	9
1	2	0	2
7	4	8	4

The procedure is, as you know, to add ones, then tens, then hundreds and then thousands; and whenever you have 10 or more in a certain column, you group.

- Add the ones: 24 ones

    24 ones = 2 tens and 4 ones
- Add the tens: 18 T's

    18 T's = 1 H and 8 T's
- Add the hundreds: 14 H's

    14 H's = 1 Th and 4 H's
- Add the thousands: 7 Th's

The answer is ___7,484___

You may, of course, do without the boxes.
Do the following additions:

a.		b.		c.		d.	
	1,204		987		1,808		4,543
	903		4,008		4,764		915
	+ 4,589		+ 3,909		+ 458		+ 2,542
	6,696		**8,904**		**7,030**		**8,000**

e.		f.		g.		h.	
	2,341		1,394		1,542		145
	1,152		1,486		014		1,274
	203		2,625		2,173		5,011
	+ 4,200		1,784		1,727		532
	7,896		+ 2,698		1,814		1,028
			9,987		+ 130		+ 1,010
					7,400		**9,000**

Add:

a.	2,151 1,082 1,193 + 1,122 **5,548**	b.	1,513 2,219 1,102 + 3,014 **7,848**	c.	1,789 897 3,014 + 2,985 **8,685**	d.	5,842 1,235 938 + 764 **8,779**
e.	631 1,472 893 2,964 + 250 **6,210**	f.	1,789 113 1,234 2,412 + 360 **5,908**	g.	2,642 1,327 1,823 1,716 + 1,531 **9,039**	h.	1,152 1,276 2,784 1,514 + 1,274 **8,000**

B

APPLICATIONS

1. The figure to the right represents a piece of land. Find the perimeter (the distance around it). (dimensions are in yards)
   <u>**6,598 yd.**</u>

$$\begin{array}{r} 1009 \\ 2060 \\ 2583 \\ +\ 946 \\ \hline 6598 \end{array}$$

2. A car dealer sold four cars for the prices shown. How much did he get for the four cars?
   <u>**$9,537**</u>

   $2,983
   $1,846
   $3,008
   $1,700

3. You subtracted 2,659 from a number. The answer was 3,948. What was the number?

   $2,659 + 3,948 = 6,607$

4. The difference between two numbers is 7,396. The smaller number is 1,006. What is the larger number?

   $7,396 + 1,006 = 8,402$

5. Add the sum of 2,954 and 1,396 to 4,008.

   a. $2,954 + 1,396 = 4,350$
   b. $4,008 + 4,350 = 8,358$

8   SUBTRACTING

Example 1.

You want to subtract: 9865 - 5213

Discussion:

1,000'S	100'S	10'S	1'S
9	8	6	5
- 5	2	1	3
4	6	5	2

- Subtract ones: 5 ones - 3 ones = 2 ones
- Subtract tens: 6 tens - 1 ten = 5 tens
- Subtract hundreds: 8 hundreds - 2 hundreds = 6 hundreds
- Subtract thousands: 9 thousands - 5 thousands = 4 thousands

Example 2.

Do the subtraction to the right.

1,000'S	100'S	10'S	1'S
6	3	9	5
- 2	6	8	2
3	7	1	3

- 5 ones - 2 ones = 3 ones
- 9 tens - 8 tens = 1 ten
- 13 H's - 6 H's = 7 H's
- 5 Th's - 2 Th's = 3 Th's

Example 3.

Do the subtraction to the right.

1,000'S	100'S	10'S	1'S
8	0	0	0
- 6	4	3	8
1	5	6	2

- 10 ones - 8 ones = 2 ones
- 9 T's - 3 T's = 6 tens
- 9 H's - 4 H's = 5 H's
- 7 Th's - 6 Th's = 1 Th

You may, of course, do without the boxes.

Do the following subtractions:

a.	8,453 - 2,421 **6,032**	b.	7,987 - 6,367 **1,620**	c.	7,165 - 1,879 **5,286**	d.	8,216 - 1,948 **6,268**
e.	8,900 - 3,465 **5,435**	f.	5,080 - 3,279 **1,801**	g.	9,040 - 6,289 **2,751**	h.	6,006 - 2,562 **3,444**
i.	8,001 - 3,068 **4,933**	j.	7,008 - 1,247 **5,761**	k.	9,000 - 3,765 **5,235**	l.	6,000 - 2,378 **3,622**

B

EXERCISES

Subtract:

a.	9,467 - 5,321 **4,146**	b.	8,358 - 1,972 **6,386**	c.	6,407 - 2,176 **4,231**	d.	9,870 - 3,289 **6,581**
e.	3,094 - 2,162 **932**	f.	5,089 - 4,327 **762**	g.	9,600 - 2,186 **7,414**	h.	8,400 - 1,715 **6,685**
i.	5,006 - 3,082 **1,924**	j.	7,009 - 6,423 **586**	k.	9,002 - 4,103 **4,899**	l.	6,001 - 2,418 **3,583**
m.	8,000 - 4,160 **3,840**	n.	9,000 - 3,750 **5,250**	o.	5,000 - 3,103 **1,897**	p.	7,000 - 2,168 **4,832**

B

APPLICATIONS

1. a. What number do you add to 1,798 for the answer to be 4,000 ?

$4,000 - 1,798 = 2,202$

   b. What number do you subtract from 6,000 for the answer to be 4,605?

$6,000 - 4,605 = 1,395$

2. a. You added 4,876 to a number. The answer was 5,000. What was the number?

$5,000 - 4,876 = 124$

   b. You subtracted 4,876 from a number. The answer was 5,000. What was the number?

$4,876 + 5,000 = 9,876$

3. The sum of two numbers is 5,678. One number is 3,765. What is the other number?

$5,678 - 3,765 = 1,913$

4. The difference between two numbers is 2,004. The larger number is 7,000. What is the smaller number?

$7,000 - 2,004 = 4,996$

5. The difference between two numbers is 2,004. The smaller number is 7,100. What is the larger number?

$7,100 + 2,004 = 9,104$

31

APPLICATIONS

1. Ted, Sue and Sam have $3,960 altogether.
   Ted has $1,250. Sam has $365 less than Ted.
   How much does Sue have?

   a. $1,250 - $365 = $885
   b. $1,250 + $885 = $2,135
   c. $3,960 - $2,135 = $1,825

2. During weekdays, a drug store sells
   235 newspapers daily.
   If 1,900 papers are sold during the 7
   days of the week, how many papers
   are sold on Sundays?

   a. 6 x 235 = 1,410
   b. 1,900 - 1,410 = 490

3. A dealer bought a car for $1,293.
   He spent $877 on repairs and
   then sold it for $2,650.
   How much profit did he make?

   a. $1,293 + $877 = $2,170
   b. $2,650 - $2,170 = $480

4. The figure to the right represents
   a piece of land. (dimensions are in yards)

   a. Find the perimeter.

   1,732 + 1,537 + 1,604 + 1,560 = 6,433 yards

   b. You want to go from A to C. How
      much distance would you save if
      you take the shortcut instead
      of going through B?

      a. 1,732 + 1,537 = 3,269 yards
      b. 3,269 - 2,704 = 565 yards

B

5. a. You added a number to 2,718.
        The answer was 6,000.
        What was the number?   6,000 - 2,718 = 3,282

    b. You subtracted a number from 8,000.
        The answer was 1,704.
        What was the number?   8,000 - 1,704 = 6,296

    c. You subtracted 3,967 from a
        number. The answer was 2,315.
        What was the number?   2,315 + 3,967 = 6,282

6. You subtracted a number from
    9,000, then added 1,384.
    The answer was 7,358.   a. 7,358 - 1,384 = 5,974
    What was the number?   b. 9,000 - 5,974 = 3,026

7. You added a number to 1,384 and
    then subtracted 4,268.
    The answer was 2,429.   a. 2,429 + 4,268 = 6,697
    What was the number?   b. 6,697 - 1,384 = 5,313

8. A is 1,965, B is 1,378 more than A,
    and C is 1,948 less than B.   a. B = 1,965 + 1,378 = 3,343
    What number is C?   b. C = 3,343 - 1,948 = 1,395

9. Study the following equation:
    N = (4 x 208) + (3 x 306)
    What number is N?   N = 832 + 918 = 1,750

10. The sum of three numbers X, Y, and Z is 9,000.   a. 4,756 + 2,563 = 7,319
    X is 4,756 and Z is 2,563. What number is Y?   b. 9,000 - 7,319 = 1,681

B

Level 12

9 MULTIPLYING BY A ONE-DIGIT NUMERAL

Example 1.

You want to multiply: 2 x 2,314

Discussion:

You may use boxes:

- 2 x 4 ones = 8 ones
- 2 x 1 ten = 2 tens
- 2 x 3 hundreds = 6 hundreds
- 2 x 2 thousands = 4 thousands

$2 \times 2,314 =$

1,000'S	100'S	10'S	1'S
4	6	2	8

$= 4,628$

Example 2.

Multiply: 3 x 2,564

Discussion:

You may use boxes:

- 3 x 4 ones = 12 ones
  12 ones = 2 ones + 1 ten
- 3 x 6 T's = 18 T's
  18 T's + 1 T = 19 T's
  19 T's = 1 H + 9 T's
- 3 x 5 H's = 15 H's
  15 H's + 1 H = 16 H's
  16 H's = 1 Th + 6 H's
- 3 x 2 Th's = 6 Th's
  6 Th's + 1 Th = 7 Th's

$3 \times 2,564 =$

1,000'S	100'S	10'S	1'S
7	6	9	2

$= 7,692$

You can, of course, do without the boxes.
Do the following multplications:

a.	3 x 2,364 = __7,092__		b.	4 x 2,065 = __8,260__
c.	6 x 1,008 = __6,048__		d.	5 x 1,876 = __9,380__
e.	2 x 4,098 = __8,196__		f.	9 x 1,019 = __9,171__
g.	3 x 3,309 = __9,927__		h.	2 x 3,987 = __7,974__
i.	4 x 2,076 = __8,304__		j.	8 x 1,202 = __9,616__

k.	l.	m.	n.
4,543 x __2__ 9,086	2,468 x __4__ 9,872	3,089 x __3__ 9,267	1,015 x __8__ 8,120

o.	p.	q.	r.
899 x __8__ 7,192	1,605 x __6__ 9,630	2,608 x __3__ 7,824	1,007 x __5__ 5,035

Level 12

Multiply:

1.
a. 2 x 1234 = __2468__
b. 4 x 2121 = __8484__
c. 8 x 1111 = __8888__
d. 3 x 2103 = __6309__
e. 5 x 1001 = __5005__
f. 4 x 2002 = __8008__
g. 3 x 1523 = __4569__
h. 6 x 1311 = __7866__
i. 7 x 1041 = __7287__
j. 9 x 834 = __7506__
k. 3 x 3015 = __9045__
l. 4 x 2105 = __8420__
m. 7 x 1024 = __7168__
n. 9 x 1005 = __9045__
o. 8 x 1051 = __8408__

2. a. 2123	b. 923	c. 1942	d. 2194
x 3	x 8	x 3	x 4
6369	7384	5826	8776
e. 1354	f. 1294	g. 785	h. 494
x 6	x 7	x 9	x 8
8124	9058	7065	3952
i. 2125	j. 1065	k. 1025	l. 1404
x 4	x 6	x 8	x 5
8500	6390	8200	7020

B

APPLICATIONS

1. One mile is 1760 yards.
   Point A is 4 miles and 890 yards
   away from point B.
   How far away is A from B in yards?

   a. 4 x 1760 = 7040
   b. 7040 + 890 = 7930

2. A drug store receives a shipment
   of 8,000 cards. 1205 boxes with
   6 cards in each box were sold.
   How many cards are still there?

   a. 1205 x 6 = 7230
   b. 8000 - 7230 = 770

3. Ted collects pennies and nickels.
   He has 1,958 pennies and 984 nickels.
   How much money does Ted have?

   a. 948 x 5¢ = 4740¢
   b. 4740¢ + 1958¢ = 6698¢
   = $66.98

4. You added a number to 3901 and
   then divided by 5. The answer
   was 878. What was the number?

   a. 878 x 5 = 4390
   b. 4390 - 3901 = 489

5. (3 x 1201) + (5 x 901) = A
   What number is A?

   3603 + 4505 = 8108

10   MULTIPLYING BY TENS OR HUNDREDS

- Suppose you have 10 long strings, with 364 beads in each string.
  Below is a picture of a part of the arrangement.
  In all how many beads are there?

Discussion:

You may see the arrangement as ten 364's, or as 364 tens.

     364 x 10 = 364 tens = 3640

So, 10 x 364 = 364 tens = 3640

Similarly:

a. 248 x 10 = __2480__	b. 907 x 10 = __9070__	c. 10 x 630 = __6300__
10 x 248 = __2480__	10 x 907 = __9070__	630 x 10 = __6300__

B

- Suppose you have 20 long strings, with 364 beads in each string.
  Below is a picture of a part of the arrangement.
  In all, how many beads are there?

Discussion:

You may see the arrangement at twenty 364's or 364 twenties.

Also you may see 364 twenties as two 364 tens.

     364 x 20 = 2 x 364 tens = 728 tens = 7280

So, 20 x 364 = 2 x 364 tens = 728 tens = 7280

Similarly:

   a.   30 x 127 = 3 x 127 tens = 381 tens = 3810

       127 x 30 = 3 x 127 tens = 381 tens = 3810

   b.   40 x 236 = 4 x 236 tens = 944 tens = 9440

       236 x 40 = 4 x 236 tens = 944 tens = 9440

- You can, of course, multiply directly:

a. 80 x 124 = __9920__	b. 40 x 205 = __8200__	c. 60 x 150 = __9000__
124 x 80 = __9920__	205 x 40 = __8200__	150 x 60 = __9000__

Multiply:

1. a. 20 x 138 = __2760__   b. 30 x 253 = __7590__   c. 80 x 121 = __9680__
   d. 60 x 132 = __7920__   e. 20 x 416 = __8320__   f. 40 x 243 = __9720__
   g. 30 x 315 = __9450__   h. 50 x 185 = __9250__   i. 60 x 109 = __6540__
   j. 80 x 112 = __8960__   k. 40 x 178 = __7120__   l. 70 x 118 = __8260__
   m. 20 x 178 = __3560__   n. 30 x 314 = __9420__   o. 20 x 419 = __8380__
   p. 40 x 215 = __8600__   q. 50 x 198 = __9900__   r. 80 x 102 = __8160__

2. a. 317 x 20 = __6340__   b. 220 x 40 = __8800__   c. 317 x 30 = __9510__
   d. 150 x 60 = __9000__   e. 386 x 20 = __7720__   f. 109 x 90 = __9810__
   g. 428 x 20 = __8560__   h. 107 x 80 = __8560__   i. 214 x 40 = __8560__
   j. 128 x 70 = __8960__   k. 294 x 30 = __8820__   l. 105 x 80 = __8400__
   m. 178 x 50 = __8900__   n. 105 x 60 = __6300__   o. 225 x 40 = __9000__
   p. 375 x 20 = __7500__   q. 270 x 30 = __8100__   r. 160 x 50 = __8000__

APPLICATIONS

1. A bank teller has 40 fifty-dollar bills and 78 one hundred-dollar bills. How much money does she have?

   40 x $50 + 78 x $100
   = $2000 + $7800 = $9800

2. A truck driver drove 30 hours at an average speed of 50 miles per hour. How many miles did he drive?

   30 x 50 = 1500

3. In the supply room there were 20 boxes with 144 pencils in each box. Now there are 960 pencils. How many pencils were given to students?

   a. 20 x 144 = 2880
   b. 2880 - 960 = 1920

4. A is 1678 and B is 200 more than 3 times A. Find the sum of A and B.

   B = (3 x 1678) + 200
   B = 5034 + 200 = 5234
   A + B = 1678 + 5234 = 6912

5. Find the answer:
   a. (30 x 195) + (13 x 200)
      5850 + 2600 = 8450

   b. (60 x 149) - (40 x 200)
      8940 - 8000 = 940

B

11 MULTIPLYING BY A TWO OR THREE-DIGIT NUMERAL

Example.

In the store room there are 28 boxes, with 144 cards in each box.
In all, how many cards are there?

Discussion:

The situation calls for the multiplication: 28 x 144.
You get the answer in 3 steps:

- 8 x 144 = 1152
- 20 x 144 = 2880
- Add   4032

You also may do the work as shown to the right.

144	144
x 28	x 28
1152	1152
2880	288
4032	4032

or

B

Do the following multiplications.

a.	b.	c.	d.
103	234	128	304
x 25	x 35	x 35	x 32
515	1170	640	608
206	702	384	912
2575	8190	4480	9728

EXERCISES

Multiply:

a.	b.	c.	d.
58	86	14	75
x 29	x 17	x 27	x 35
522	602	98	375
116	86	28	225
1682	1462	378	2625

e.	f.	g.	h.
164	293	319	225
x 24	x 18	x 26	x 25
656	2344	1914	1125
328	293	638	450
3936	5274	8294	5625

i.	j.	k.	l.
309	103	201	302
x 29	x 23	x 29	x 24
2781	309	1809	1208
618	206	402	604
8961	2369	5829	7248

APPLICATIONS

1. You have 35 quarters.
   How much money do you have?

   $\underline{35 \times 25¢ = 875¢ = \$8.75}$

2. You need 18¢ more than you have
   in order to buy 24 pens at 29¢ each.
   How much money do you have?

   a. $\underline{24 \times 29¢ = 696¢}$
   b. $\underline{696¢ - 18¢ = 678¢ = \$6.78}$

3. One week, a farmer sold 128 dozen
   eggs. How many eggs did he sell?

   $\underline{128 \times 12 = 1536}$

4. On a vacation, a family drove 25 hours
   at a speed of 48 miles per hour.
   How many miles did the family drive?

   $\underline{25 \times 48 = 1200}$

5. John takes home \$736 a month.
   He saves \$1270 a year.
   How much does he spend in a year?

   a. $\underline{12 \times \$736 = \$8832}$
   b. $\underline{\$8832 - \$1270 = \$7562}$

6. You divide a number by 38.
   The answer was 79.
   What was the number?

   $\underline{38 \times 79 = 3002}$

7. Find the answer:

a. (48 x 105) - 2384	b. 7900 - (38 x 49)
$\underline{5040 - 2384 = 2656}$	$\underline{7900 - 1862 = 6038}$
c. (65 x 49) - (25 x 104)	d. (89 x 54) - (68 x 51)
$\underline{3185 - 2600 = 585}$	$\underline{4806 - 3468 = 1338}$

B

Level 12

12 DIVIDING BY A ONE-DIGIT NUMERAL

Example 1.
  Do the division to the right:
  • 6 Thousands ÷ 3 = 2 Thousands
  • 3 Hundreds ÷ 3 = 1 Hundred
  • 0 Tens ÷ 3 = 0 Tens
  • 9 Ones ÷ 3 = 3 Ones

$$\frac{2,103}{3)6,309}$$

Example 2.
  Do the division to the right:
  • 7 Th's ÷ 5 = 1 Th, and 2 Th's remain.
  • 23 H's ÷ 5 = 4 H's, and 3 H's remain.
  • 39 T's ÷ 5 = 7 T's, and 4 T's remain.
  • 45 Ones ÷ 5 = 9 Ones

$$\frac{1,479}{5)7,395}$$

B

EXERCISES

Divide:

a. $\frac{1,111}{7)7,777}$	b. $\frac{1,321}{3)3,963}$	c. $\frac{2,112}{4)8,448}$	d. $\frac{2,413}{2)4,826}$
e. $\frac{2,031}{3)6,093}$	f. $\frac{2,001}{4)8,004}$	g. $\frac{1,001}{5)5,005}$	h. $\frac{4,213}{2)8,426}$
i. $\frac{1,624}{2)3,248}$	j. $\frac{1,915}{5)9,575}$	k. $\frac{1,127}{8)9,016}$	l. $\frac{1,618}{4)6,472}$
m. $\frac{1,033}{8)8,264}$	n. $\frac{1,067}{5)5,335}$	o. $\frac{0,906}{6)5,436}$	p. $\frac{0,302}{9)2,718}$
q. $\frac{950}{4)3,800}$	r. $\frac{3,017}{3)9,051}$	s. $\frac{901}{7)6,307}$	t. $\frac{1,060}{6)6,360}$
u. $\frac{1,699}{5)8,495}$	v. $\frac{2,092}{4)8,368}$	w. $\frac{2,098}{3)6,294}$	x. $\frac{375}{8)3,000}$

APPLICATIONS

1. a. How many yards are in 7,002 feet?

    a. $7,002 \div 3 = 2,334$

    b. How many gallons are in 8,176 pints?

    b. $8,176 \div 8 = 1,022$

2. Tom had 7 boxes with 935 pennies in each box.
    He exchanged them for nickels.
    How many nickels did he get?

    a. $7 \times 935 = 6,545$
    b. $6,545 \div 5 = 1,309$

3. During 6 days, 3,042 individuals used
    the public library.
    What is the average number of individuals
    who used the library per day?

    $3,042 \div 6 = 507$

4. In 5 months Tom and his family covered
    8,735 miles.
    What is the average distance they
    covered monthly?

    $8,735 \div 5 = 1,747$ miles

5. You subtracted 3,872 from a number,
    and then multiplied by 4.
    The answer was 9,204.
    What was the number?

    a. $9,204 \div 4 = 2,301$
    b. $3,872 + 2,301 = 6,173$

6. You subtracted a number from 9,000
    and then multiplied by 3.
    The answer was 8,412.
    What was the number?

    a. $8,412 \div 3 = 2,804$
    b. $9,000 - 2,804 = 6,196$

7. You started with a number. You added
    2,398, then divided by 7.
    The answer was 853.
    What was the number?

    a. $853 \times 7 = 5,971$
    b. $5,971 - 2,398 = 3,573$

8. Study the following equation:
    N = 9,000 - (9,010 ÷ 5)

    What number is N?

    $N = 9,000 - 1,802 = 7,198$

Level 12

B

13   ESTIMATING THE ANSWER

Example 1.
    In the division to the right,
    what is the answer?

$$\begin{array}{r} 004 \\ 35\overline{)140} \end{array}$$

Discussion:
- The answer is not 0.
     Why?   Because 0 x 35 = 0
- The answer is not 10.
     Why?   Because 10 x 35 = 350
- Is the answer 1, 2, 3, 4, 5, 6, 7, 8, or 9?   __4__

Example 2.
    In the division to the right,
    what is the answer?

$$\begin{array}{r} 009 \\ 85\overline{)765} \end{array}$$

Discussion:
- The answer is not 0.
     Why?   Because 0 x 85 = 0
- The answer is not 10.
     Why?   Because 10 x 85 = 850
- Is the answer 1, 2, 3, 4, 5, 6, 7, 8, or 9?   __9__

EXERCISES

Divide:

a. $\begin{array}{r}005\\57\overline{)285}\\285\end{array}$	b. $\begin{array}{r}009\\79\overline{)711}\\711\end{array}$	c. $\begin{array}{r}008\\96\overline{)768}\\768\end{array}$	d. $\begin{array}{r}005\\138\overline{)690}\\690\end{array}$
e. $\begin{array}{r}004\\238\overline{)952}\\952\end{array}$	f. $\begin{array}{r}003\\584\overline{)1,752}\\1752\end{array}$	g. $\begin{array}{r}005\\624\overline{)3,120}\\3,120\end{array}$	h. $\begin{array}{r}004\\415\overline{)1,660}\\1,660\end{array}$
i. $\begin{array}{r}009\\603\overline{)5,427}\\5,427\end{array}$	j. $\begin{array}{r}008\\248\overline{)1,984}\\1,984\end{array}$	k. $\begin{array}{r}005\\515\overline{)2,575}\\2,575\end{array}$	l. $\begin{array}{r}006\\316\overline{)1,896}\\1,896\end{array}$
m. $\begin{array}{r}007\\309\overline{)2,163}\\2,163\end{array}$	n. $\begin{array}{r}009\\717\overline{)6,453}\\6,453\end{array}$	o. $\begin{array}{r}007\\410\overline{)2,870}\\2,870\end{array}$	p. $\begin{array}{r}009\\190\overline{)1,710}\\1,710\end{array}$

As you divide, there may be a remainder as shown:

a.	b.	c.
$$\frac{005}{85)498}$$ $$\frac{425}{73}$$	$$\frac{0\ 003}{392)1,248}$$ $$\frac{1,176}{72}$$	$$\frac{0\ 008}{350)2,924}$$ $$\frac{2,800}{124}$$
The answer is 5, R73	The answer is ___3, R72___	The answer is ___8, R124___

EXERCISES

Divide:

a.	b.	c.	d.
$$\frac{005}{74)435}$$ $$\frac{370}{65}$$	$$\frac{005}{98)568}$$ $$\frac{490}{78}$$	$$\frac{005}{39)204}$$ $$\frac{195}{9}$$	$$\frac{006}{46)289}$$ $$\frac{276}{13}$$
e.	f.	g.	h.
$$\frac{008}{75)605}$$ $$\frac{600}{5}$$	$$\frac{006}{125)797}$$ $$\frac{750}{47}$$	$$\frac{007}{158)1,158}$$ $$\frac{1,106}{52}$$	$$\frac{004}{512)2,176}$$ $$\frac{2,048}{128}$$
i.	j.	k.	l.
$$\frac{007}{450)3,158}$$ $$\frac{3,150}{8}$$	$$\frac{005}{294)1,674}$$ $$\frac{1,470}{204}$$	$$\frac{009}{604)5,894}$$ $$\frac{5,436}{458}$$	$$\frac{006}{560)3,548}$$ $$\frac{3,360}{188}$$
m.	n.	o.	p.
$$\frac{003}{790)2,891}$$ $$\frac{2,370}{521}$$	$$\frac{002}{890)2,148}$$ $$\frac{1,780}{368}$$	$$\frac{007}{298)2,156}$$ $$\frac{2,086}{70}$$	$$\frac{009}{428)4,164}$$ $$\frac{3,852}{312}$$
q.	r.	s.	t.
$$\frac{005}{565)2,948}$$ $$\frac{2,825}{123}$$	$$\frac{003}{584)2,000}$$ $$\frac{1,752}{248}$$	$$\frac{007}{970)6,940}$$ $$\frac{6,790}{150}$$	$$\frac{007}{381)2,680}$$ $$\frac{2,667}{13}$$

B

43

14 DIVIDING BY A TWO OR THREE-DIGIT NUMERAL

Example 1.

Do the division to the right.

Step by step:

- 1 Th ÷ 25 = 0 Th, 1 Th remains.
- 13 H's ÷ 25 = 0 H's, 13 H's remain.
- 132 T's ÷ 25 = 5 T's, 7 T's remain.
- 75 Ones ÷ 25 = 3 Ones.

$$\begin{array}{r} 0053 \\ 25)\overline{1325} \\ \underline{1250} \\ 75 \\ \underline{75} \end{array}$$

Example 2.

Do the division to the right.

Step by step:

- 9Th's ÷ 248 = 0 Th, 9 Th's remain.
- 91 H's ÷ 248 = 0 H's, 91 H's remain.
- 917T's ÷ 248 = 3 T's, 173 T's remain.
- 1736 ones ÷ 248 = 7 ones.

$$\begin{array}{r} 0037 \\ 248)\overline{9176} \\ \underline{7440} \\ 1736 \\ \underline{1736} \end{array}$$

EXERCISES

Divide:

a.	b.	c.	d.
$\begin{array}{r} 0072 \\ 25)\overline{1800} \\ \underline{175} \\ 50 \\ \underline{50} \end{array}$	$\begin{array}{r} 0014 \\ 76)\overline{1064} \\ \underline{760} \\ 304 \\ \underline{304} \end{array}$	$\begin{array}{r} 0064 \\ 125)\overline{8000} \\ \underline{750} \\ 500 \\ \underline{500} \end{array}$	$\begin{array}{r} 0012 \\ 86)\overline{1032} \\ \underline{86} \\ 172 \\ \underline{172} \end{array}$
e.	f.	g.	h.
$\begin{array}{r} 0037 \\ 89)\overline{3293} \\ \underline{267} \\ 623 \\ \underline{623} \end{array}$	$\begin{array}{r} 0046 \\ 130)\overline{5980} \\ \underline{520} \\ 780 \\ \underline{780} \end{array}$	$\begin{array}{r} 0028 \\ 75)\overline{2100} \\ \underline{150} \\ 600 \\ \underline{600} \end{array}$	$\begin{array}{r} 0052 \\ 170)\overline{8840} \\ \underline{850} \\ 340 \\ \underline{340} \end{array}$
i.	j.	k.	l.
$\begin{array}{r} 0024 \\ 126)\overline{3024} \\ \underline{252} \\ 504 \\ \underline{504} \end{array}$	$\begin{array}{r} 0037 \\ 245)\overline{9065} \\ \underline{735} \\ 1715 \\ \underline{1715} \end{array}$	$\begin{array}{r} 0015 \\ 418)\overline{6270} \\ \underline{418} \\ 2090 \\ \underline{2090} \end{array}$	$\begin{array}{r} 0026 \\ 315)\overline{8190} \\ \underline{630} \\ 1890 \\ \underline{1890} \end{array}$

Divide:

a.	b.	c.	d.
0155 25) 3875 25 137 125 125 125	0541 12) 6492 60 49 48 12 12	0226 35) 7910 70 91 70 210 210	0315 26) 8190 78 39 26 130 130

e.	f.	g.	h.
182 32) 5824 32 262 256 64 64	216 45) 9720 90 72 45 270 270	0049 28) 1372 112 252 252	0041 64) 2624 256 64 64

i.	j.	k.	l.
0064 57) 3648 342 228 228	0025 125) 3125 250 625 625	0016 225) 3600 225 1350 1350	0028 125) 3500 250 1000 1000

m.	n.	o.	p.
0025 368) 9342 736 1982 1840 142	0036 138) 5000 4140 860 828 32	0064 125) 8010 7500 510 500 10	0022 251) 5684 502 664 502 162

The following divisions need special attention:

a. $$\begin{array}{r} 0040 \\ 78\overline{)3120} \\ \underline{312} \end{array}$$	b. $$\begin{array}{r} 0030 \\ 69\overline{)2070} \\ \underline{207} \end{array}$$	c. $$\begin{array}{r} 0060 \\ 84\overline{)5040} \\ \underline{504} \end{array}$$	d. $$\begin{array}{r} 0060 \\ 145\overline{)8700} \\ \underline{870} \end{array}$$
e. $$\begin{array}{r} 200 \\ 43\overline{)8627} \\ \underline{86} \\ 27 \end{array}$$	f. $$\begin{array}{r} 300 \\ 25\overline{)7512} \\ \underline{75} \\ 12 \end{array}$$	g. $$\begin{array}{r} 200 \\ 39\overline{)7815} \\ \underline{78} \\ 15 \end{array}$$	h. $$\begin{array}{r} 0400 \\ 23\overline{)9200} \\ \underline{92} \end{array}$$
i. $$\begin{array}{r} 170 \\ 45\overline{)7650} \\ \underline{45} \\ 315 \\ \underline{315} \end{array}$$	j. $$\begin{array}{r} 0270 \\ 24\overline{)6480} \\ \underline{48} \\ 168 \\ \underline{168} \end{array}$$	k. $$\begin{array}{r} 120 \\ 26\overline{)3120} \\ \underline{26} \\ 52 \\ \underline{52} \end{array}$$	l. $$\begin{array}{r} 150 \\ 32\overline{)4800} \\ \underline{32} \\ 160 \\ \underline{160} \end{array}$$
m. $$\begin{array}{r} 0105 \\ 37\overline{)3885} \\ \underline{37} \\ 185 \\ \underline{185} \end{array}$$	n. $$\begin{array}{r} 0301 \\ 25\overline{)7525} \\ \underline{75} \\ 25 \\ \underline{25} \end{array}$$	o. $$\begin{array}{r} 0305 \\ 26\overline{)7930} \\ \underline{78} \\ 130 \\ \underline{130} \end{array}$$	p. $$\begin{array}{r} 204 \\ 46\overline{)9384} \\ \underline{92} \\ 184 \\ \underline{184} \end{array}$$
q. $$\begin{array}{r} 40 \\ 127\overline{)5094} \\ \underline{508} \\ 14 \end{array}$$	r. $$\begin{array}{r} 0400 \\ 24\overline{)9617} \\ \underline{96} \\ 17 \end{array}$$	s. $$\begin{array}{r} 0140 \\ 28\overline{)3920} \\ \underline{28} \\ 112 \\ \underline{112} \end{array}$$	t. $$\begin{array}{r} 0209 \\ 35\overline{)7340} \\ \underline{70} \\ 340 \\ \underline{315} \\ 25 \end{array}$$

B

APPLICATIONS

1. a. You want to divide 3490 items into
        sets with 125 items in each set.
        What is the result?

        <u>27 sets are made and 115 items remain</u>

    b. You want to divide 3490 items equally
        into 125 sets.
        What is the result?

        <u>27 items in each set and 115 items remain</u>

```
        27
125) 3490
     250
     990
     875
     115
```

2. Mr. Hills has 250 dozens of eggs,
    in boxes with 75 eggs in each box.
    How many boxes has he used?

    a. <u>250 x 12 = 3000</u>
    b. <u>3000 ÷ 75 = 40</u>

3. a. How many quarters do you
        exchange for 190 dimes?

        a. <u>190 x 10 = 1900</u>
        b. <u>1900 ÷ 25 = 76</u>

    b. How many dimes do you
        exchange for 180 quarters?

        a. <u>180 x 25 = 4500</u>
        b. <u>4500 ÷ 10 = 450</u>

4. a. You multiplied a number by 54.
        The answer was 4806.
        What was the number?

```
        0089
54) 4806
    432
    486
    486
```

    b. 128 times N is 3200.
        What number is N?

```
        0025
128) 3200
     256
     640
     640
```

5. What number do you add to the sum of
    1940 and 2760 to make it divisible by 39?   <u>19</u>

```
        0120
39) 4700
    39
    80
    78
    20
```

Level 12

B

15 WHAT IS THE NUMBER?

1. a. You added 5,342 to a number.
    The answer was 8,001.
    What was the number?

    $8,001 - 5,342 = 2,659$

    b. You added a number to 1,432.
    The answer was 4,090.
    What was the number?

    $4,090 - 1,432 = 2,658$

2. a. You subtracted a number from
    5,000. The answer was 2,306.
    What was the number?

    $5,000 - 2,306 = 2,694$

    b. You subtracted 3,504 from
    a number. The answer was 2,967.
    What was the number?

    $3,504 + 2,967 = 6,471$

3. a. You multiplied a number by 27.
    The answer was 3348.
    What was the number?

    $$\begin{array}{r} 0124 \\ 27\overline{)3348} \\ 27 \\ \hline 64 \\ 54 \\ \hline 108 \\ 108 \\ \hline \end{array}$$

    b. You multiplied 38 by a number.
    The answer was 2470
    What was the number?

    $$\begin{array}{r} 0065 \\ 38\overline{)2470} \\ 228 \\ \hline 190 \\ 190 \\ \hline \end{array}$$

4. a. You divided a number by 25.
    The answer was 125.
    What was the number?

    $$\begin{array}{r} 125 \\ \times\ 25 \\ \hline 625 \\ 250 \\ \hline 3125 \end{array}$$

    b. You divided 3250 by a number.
    The answer was 125.
    What was the number?

    $$\begin{array}{r} 0026 \\ 125\overline{)3250} \\ 250 \\ \hline 750 \\ 750 \\ \hline \end{array}$$

5. a. You divided a number by 36.
    The answer was 59 and
    a remainder of 26.
    What was the number?

    a. $36 \times 59 = 2124$
    b. $2124 + 26 = 2150$

    b. You divided 5420 by a number.
    The answer was 60 and
    a remainder of 20.
    What was the number?

    a. $5420 - 20 = 5400$
    b. $5400 \div 60 = 90$

6. The sum of 98 and N is 3409.
   What number is N?

   $3409 - 98 = 3311$

7. The product of 68 and X is 2516.
   What number is X?

   $$\begin{array}{r} 0037 \\ 68)\overline{2516} \\ 204 \\ \hline 476 \\ 476 \end{array}$$

8. In a division, the dividend is 3000.
   and the quotient is 75.
   What was the divisor?

   $$\begin{array}{r} 0040 \\ 75)\overline{3000} \\ 3000 \end{array}$$

9. In a division, the divisor is 65, and
   the answer is 24 and a remainder of 18.
   What is the dividend?

   a. $65 \times 24 = 1560$
   b. $1560 + 18 = 1578$

10. The difference between 2010 and A is 1070.
    There are two values for A.
    What are they?

    $2010 + 1070 = 3080$
    or $2010 - 1070 = 940$

11. a. What is the smallest number you
       subtract from 9753 to make the
       number divisible by 25?
    b. What is the smallest number you add
       to 9753 to make the answer divisible by 25?

    $$\begin{array}{r} 0390 \\ 25)\overline{9753} \\ 75 \\ \hline 225 \\ 225 \\ \hline 3 \end{array}$$

    3

    22

12. N - (10 x 300) = 4000
    What number is N?

    a. $N - 3000 = 4000$
    b. $N = 4000 + 3000 = 7000$

13. A + (20 x 400) = 9000
    What number is A?

    a. $A + 8000 = 9000$
    b. $A = 9000 - 8000 = 1000$

14. You multiplied a number by 25, and then
    added 3000. The answer was 7000.
    What was the number?

    a. $7000 - 3000 = 4000$
    b. $4000 \div 25 = 160$

15. You added 1728 to a number and then
    divided by 25. The answer was 364.
    What was the number?

    a. $364 \times 25 = 9100$
    b. $9100 - 1728 = 7372$

B

WHAT IS THE NUMBER?

1. a. You multiplied a number by 25.
   The answer was 375.
   What was the number?

   ```
        015
   25) 375
       25
      125
      125
   ```

   b. You divided a number by 25.
   The answer was 375.
   What was the number?

   ```
      375
   x   25
     1875
      750
     9375
   ```

2. a. The sum of two numbers is 3850.
   One number is 35.
   What is the other number?

   ```
     3850
   -   35
     3815
   ```

   b. The product of two numbers is 3850.
   One number is 35.
   What is the other number?

   ```
         0110
   35)3850
         35
         35
         35
   ```

3. a. The difference between 2768 and
   a larger number is 2648.
   What is the number?

   ```
     2768
   + 2648
     5416
   ```

   b. The difference between 2768 and
   a smaller number is 2648.
   What is the number?

   ```
     2768
   - 2648
      120
   ```

4. a. What number do you add to 7678
   for the answer to be 9000?

   ```
     9000
   - 7678
     1322
   ```

   b. What number do you subtract from
   6125 for the answer to be 5694?

   ```
     6125
   - 5694
      431
   ```

5. a. In the division to the right,
   what number is missing?

   ```
     238          0039
   x  39      238)
    2142
     714
    9282
   ```

   b. In the division to the right,
   what number is missing?

   ```
            0122
        0076   ) 9272
   122)9272
        854
        732
        732
   ```

6. The sum of 1837, 2634, and N is 7000.
   What number is N?

   a. $1837 + 2634 = 4471$
   b. $7000 - 4471 = 2529$

7. You multiplied a number by 25, and then
   added 2368. The answer was 7143.
   What was the number?

   a. $7143 - 2368 = 4775$
   b. $4775 \div 25 = 191$

8. You divided a number by 239.
   There was a remainder.
   a. What is the lowest number the remainder may be?   1
   b. What is the highest number the remainder may be?   238

9. You multiplied a number by 24,
   and then multiplied by 12.
   The answer was 4320.
   What was the number?

   a. $4320 \div 12 = 360$
   b. $360 \div 24 = 15$

10. You divided a number by 49, and
    then multiplied the quotient by 34.
    The answer was 3060.
    What was the number?

    a. $3060 \div 34 = 90$
    b. $90 \times 49 = 4100$

11. $N - 3000 = 70 \times 40$
    What number is N?

    a. $N - 3000 = 2800$
    b. $N = 2800 + 3000 = 5800$

12. $9000 - X = 18 \times 500$
    What number is X?

    a. $9000 - X = 9000$
    b. $X = 9000 - 9000 = 0$

B

Level 12

WHAT IS THE NUMBER?

1. The sum of 1387 and N is 6000.
   What number is N?

   $N = 6000 - 1387 = 4613$

2. The sum of 3879, 2412, and A is 9048.
   What number is A?

   a. $3879 + 2412 = 6291$
   b. $9048 - 6291 = 2757$

3. $A = 25 \times 38$
   $B = 36 \times 49$
   What number is the sum of A and B?

   a. $A = 950$
   b. $B = 1764$
   c. $A + B = 2714$

4. $M = 7500 \div 25$
   $N = 3800 \div 190$
   What is the product of M and N?

   a. $M = 7500 \div 25 = 300$
   b. $N = 3800 \div 190 = 20$
   c. $M \times N = 300 \times 20 = 6000$

5. M, N, and T are three numbers.
   Given that M is 3978, N is 2000 less than
   M, and T is 1804 more than N.
   a. What number is N?

   $N = 3978 - 2000 = 1978$

   b. What number is T?

   $T = 1978 + 1804 = 3782$

6. a. $100 \times$ a number $= 8000$
      What is the number?

   a. $8000 \div 100 = 80$

   b. A number $\times 10 = 7500$
      What is the number?

   b. $7500 \div 10 = 750$

7. a. $3500 \div N = 70$
      What number is N?

   $N = 3500 \div 70 = 50$

   b. $X \div 56 = 24$
      What number is X?

   $X = 56 \times 24 = 1344$

8. You added 3700 to twice a number.
   The answer was 6000.
   What was the number?

   a. $6000 - 3700 = 2300$
   b. $2300 \div 2 = 1150$

9. You subtracted 2600 from 3 times a number.
   The answer was 7000.
   What was the number?

   a. $7000 + 2600 = 9600$
   b. $9600 \div 3 = 3200$

10. a. What number do you subtract from 8984
       for the answer to be divisible by 125?
    b. What number do you add to 8984 for
       the answer to be divisible by 125?

$$\begin{array}{r} 0071 \\ 125\overline{)8984} \\ 875 \\ \hline 234 \\ 125 \\ \hline 109 \end{array}$$

   109

   16

11. You added the product of 27 and 65
    to 1796.
    What was the answer?

    a. $27 \times 65 = 1755$
    b. $1755 + 1796 = 3551$

12. $N + (75 \times 38) = 6000$
    What number is N?

    a. $N + 2850 = 6000$
    b. $N = 6000 + 2850 = 3150$

13. $X - (36 \times 49) = 1000$
    What number is X?

    a. $X - 1764 = 1000$
    b. $X = 1764 + 1000 = 2764$

14. $(3 \times A) + 7000 = 9700$
    What number is A?

    a. $(3 \times A) = 9700 - 7000 = 2700$
    b. $A = 2700 \div 3 = 900$

15. $(5 \times B) - 1500 = 2400$
    What number is B?

    a. $(5 \times B) = 2400 + 1500 = 3900$
    b. $B = 3900 \div 5 = 780$

B

UNIT B TEST

1. How much money is pictured below?

     $2,103

    $1,002

2. Write numerals for:
   a. 3 Th's, 6 H's, 5 T's, and 8 ones   3658
   b. 6 Th's, and 7 ones   6007
   c. 4 Th's, and 3 tens   4030
   d. 2 Th's, and 9 H's   2900

3. Add:

a.	b.	c.	d.
3,214	1,761	1,389	2,157
1,602	2,902	2,678	1,292
1,151	1,613	1,984	1,346
+ 2,012	+ 1,423	+ 1,815	1,525
7,979	**7,699**	**7,866**	+ 1,680
			8,000

4. Subtract:

a.	b.	c.	d.
5,083	6,008	7,005	9,000
- 2,529	- 4,872	- 3,209	- 3,584
2,554	**1,136**	**3,796**	**5,416**

5. Ted had $3,925. Dan has $765 more than Ted. How much do they both have altogether?

   a. $3,925 + $765 = $4,690
   b. $4,690 + $3,925 = $8,615

6. A dealer bought two cars, one for $2,475 and the other for $3,150. He sold each car for $3,025.
   a. How much did he make on the first car? $3,025 - $2,475 = $550
   b. How much did he lose on the second car? $3,150 - $3,025 = $125

7. The difference between 968 and a larger number N is 1,697. Find the sum of the two numbers.

   a. N = 968 + 1,697 = 2,665
   b. 2,665 + 968 = 3,633

8. Fill in the boxes:

1,000'S	100'S	10'S	1'S
5	3	5	2

$3 \times 1,784 = $

9. Multiply:
   a. $2 \times 2,134 = $ __4,268__
   c. $5 \times 1,241 = $ __6,205__

   b. $6 \times 1,312 = $ __7,872__
   d. $8 \times 1,125 = $ __9,000__

e.	985	f.	2,148	g.	1,059
	x 9		x 4		x 8
	8,865		8,592		8,472

10. Multiply:
    a. $10 \times 764 = $ __7640__
    c. $20 \times 397 = $ __7940__
    e. $50 \times 196 = $ __9800__

    b. $968 \times 10 = $ __9680__
    d. $148 \times 60 = $ __8880__
    f. $225 \times 40 = $ __9000__

11. Multiply:

a.	49	b.	36	c.	125
	x 67		x 59		x 58
	343		324		1000
	294		180		625
	3283		2124		7250

12. A builder bought 4 pieces of land
    for $1,975 each, and sold them
    all for $9,500.
    How much profit did he make?

    a. $4 \times \$1,975 = \$7,900$
    b. $\$9,500 - \$7,900 = \$1,600$

13. In the supply room, there are 20 boxes with
    48 crayons in each box, and 30 boxes with
    25 crayons in each box.
    How many crayons are there?

    a. $20 \times 48 = 960$
    b. $30 \times 25 = 750$
    c. Total $= 1,710$

14. You had 23 boxes with 96 stamps in each box.
    You sold 1293 stamps.
    How many stamps do you have left?

    a. $23 \times 96 = 2,208$
    b. $2,208 - 1,293 = 915$

15. $A + 7,000 = 20 \times 460$
    What number is A?

    a. $A + 7,000 = 9,200$
    b. $A = 9,200 - 7,000 = 2,200$

B

16. Divide:

a. $9,369 \div 3 =$ ___3,123___

b. $7,842 \div 2 =$ ___3,921___

c. $3,052 \div 4 =$ ___763___

d. $9,005 \div 5 =$ ___1,801___

e. $3,094 \div 7 =$ ___442___

f. $6,012 \div 8 =$ ___751 R4___

g.
$$\frac{3,102}{3)9,306}$$

h.
$$\frac{1,585}{5)7,925}$$

i.
$$\frac{807\ R1}{7)5,650}$$

17. Divide:

a.
$$\frac{0005}{425)\,2125}$$
$$\underline{2125}$$

b.
$$\frac{0006}{273)\,1671}$$
$$\underline{1638}$$
$$33$$

c.
$$\frac{0003}{932)\,2850}$$
$$\underline{2796}$$
$$54$$

18. Divide:

a.
$$\frac{0023}{45)\,1035}$$
$$\underline{90}$$
$$135$$
$$\underline{135}$$

b.
$$\frac{0055}{125)\,6925}$$
$$\underline{625}$$
$$675$$
$$\underline{625}$$
$$50$$

c.
$$\frac{0306}{25)\,7650}$$
$$\underline{750}$$
$$150$$
$$\underline{150}$$

19. a. You had 3600 stamps.
You divided them equally into 45 sets.
What was the result?

$$\frac{0080}{45)\,3600}$$
$$\underline{360}$$

___80 stamps in each set___

b. You had 2100 stamps.
You made them into sets with 14 stamps
in each set.
What was the result?

$$\frac{0150}{14)\,2100}$$
$$\underline{14}$$
$$70$$
$$\underline{70}$$

___150 sets were made___

20. For a concert, 234 tickets were
sold for the total price of $3510.
How much was the price of 1 ticket?

$$\frac{0015}{234)\,3510}$$
$$\underline{234}$$
$$1170$$
$$\underline{1170}$$

21. How many quarters do you get for 360 dimes?

a. $360 \times 10 = 3600$

b. $3600 \div 25 = 144$

22. a. The sum of A and 3,984 is 9,000. What number is A?

$9,000 - 3,984 = 5,016$

b. The product of 38 and another number is 1,900. What is the number?

$1900 \div 38 = 50$

23. a. The difference between 2,008 and a smaller number X is 1,394. What number is X?

$2,008 - 1,394 = 614$

b. The difference between 3,084 and a larger number N is 2,648. What number is N?

$3,084 + 2,648 = 5,732$

24. a. In a division, the divisor is 73, and the quotient is 34. What is the dividend?

$73 \times 34 = 2482$

b. In a division, the divisor is 56, the quotient is 23, and the remainder is 15. What is the dividend?

a. $56 \times 23 = 1288$
b. $1288 + 15 = 1303$

c. In a division, the dividend is 2,015, the quotient is 80, and the remainder is 15. What is the divisor?

a. $2015 - 15 = 2000$
b. $2000 \div 80 = 25$

25. a. What number do you subtract from 1600 for the answer to be divisible by 85?

$$
\begin{array}{r}
70 \\
\end{array}
\qquad
\begin{array}{r}
0018 \\
85)\overline{1600} \\
\underline{85} \\
750 \\
\underline{680} \\
70
\end{array}
$$

b. What number do you add to 1600 for the answer to be divisible by 85?

15

26. You multiplied a number by 28, and then added 29. The answer was 3529. What was the number?

a. $3529 - 29 = 3500$
b. $3500 \div 28 = 125$

B

Level 12

- Numeral A is read,
    "three hundred ninety-seven"
- Number B is read,
    "two hundred eighty-six thousands"

ONES		
100'S	10'S	1'S
3	9	7

A

THOUSANDS		
100'S	10'S	1'S
2	8	6

B

- If you add the two numbers, a six-place number is created. It is read, "two hundred eighty-six thousand three hundred ninety-seven.", and is written 286,397

THOUSANDS			ONES		
100'S	10'S	1'S	100'S	10'S	1'S
2	8	6	3	9	7

- 286,397 is the same as:
    $200,000 + 80,000 + 6,000 + 300 + 90 + 7$

Similarly:

a. $542,368 = 500,000 + 40,000 + 2,000 + 300 + 60 + 8$
b. $206,795 = 200,000 + 6,000 + 700 + 90 + 5$
c. $980,243 = \underline{900,000 + 80,000 + 200 + 40 + 3}$
d. $490,005 = \underline{400,000 + 90,000 + 5}$
e. $100,076 = \underline{100,000 + 70 + 6}$

- You know that the value of a digit depends on the place it occupies in the numeral.

Example 1.

In the numeral 428,576:

THOUSANDS			ONES		
100'S	10'S	1'S	100'S	10'S	1'S
4	2	8	5	7	6

- the 7 has a value of 7 tens.
- the 2 has a value of 2 tens of thousands.
- the 5 has a value of 5 hundreds.
- the 4 has a value of 4 hundreds of thousands.
- the 8 has a value of 8 thousands.
- the 6 has a value of 6 ones.

Example 2.

In the numeral 629,078

- the 7 has a value of __7 tens__
- the 8 has a value of __8 ones__
- the 2 has a value of __2 tens of thousands__
- the 9 has a value of __9 thousands__
- the 6 has a value of __6 hundreds of thousands__

APPLICATIONS

1. Write numerals for:
   a. 5 tens, 3 thousands, 9 ones, 6 hundreds of thousands, 8 hundreds.   603,859
   b. 7 thousands, 9 hundreds, 7 tens of thousands, 8 ones.   77,908
   c. 6 hundreds of thousands, 8 hundreds.   600,800
   d. 9 tens of thousands, 7 ones.   90,007

2. Write numerals for:
   a. $800,000 + 90,000 + 6,000 + 700 + 50 + 4$ 896,754
   b. $7 + 80 + 400 + 9,000 + 60,000 + 100,000$ 169,487
   c. $600,000 + 9,000 + 800$ 609,800
   d. $100 + 100,000 + 1$ 100,101
   e. $3,000 + 30 + 300,000$ 303,030

3. a. What number is 600 more than 600,000?   600,600
   b. What number is 7 more than 274,000?   274,007
   c. What number is 35 more than 501,000?   501,035
   d. What number is 834 more than 834,000?   834,834

4. a. What is the largest 5 place number?   99,999
   b. What is the smallest 5 place number?   10,000
   c. What is the largest 6 place number?   999,999
   d. What is the smallest 6 place number?   100,000

5. a. Use the digits 8, 3, 2, 5, and 6 to form the largest number you can.   86,532
   b. Use the same digits to form the smallest number you can.   23,568

6. a. Use the digits 1, 2, 5, 0, 9 and 8 to form the largest number you can form.   985,210
   b. Use the digits 0, 8, 5, 3, 2 and 1 to form the smallest number you can form.   012,358

Level 12

17 ADDING AND SUBTRACTING

You know that to add a column of numbers, you add the digits in each column, starting with the ones.

You may also know that if the sum of the digits in any column is 10 or more, you must group.

Example:

- Add the ones: 19

    19 ones must be grouped into 1 ten and 9 ones.
- Add the tens: 7

    No grouping is involved.
- Add the hundreds: 18

    18 hundreds must be grouped into 1 Th and 8 H's
- Add the thousands: 26

    26 Th's must be grouped into 2 T's of Th's, and 6 Th's.
- Add the tens of thousands: 20

    20 T's of Th's must be grouped into 2 H's of Th's and 0T's of Th's
- Add the hundreds of thousands: 7

237,613
179,427
105,534
+ 184,305
706,879

Do the following additions:

a.	b.	c.	d.
94,867	65,167	26,121	113,452
18,958	179,283	110,043	365,121
26,796	34,335	254,487	197,133
+ 45,847	+ 218,019	+ 81,149	+ 24,294
186,468	496,804	471,800	700,000

You know that to subtract a number from another, you start with the ones, then the tens, then the hundreds, ... etc.

You also know that sometimes the subtraction involves exchanging.

Example:

- 11 ones - 7 ones = 4 ones
- 12 tens - 4 tens = 8 tens
- 15 H's - 9 H's = 6 H's
- 14 Th's - 8 Th's = 6 Th's
- 11 T's of Th's - 7 T's of Th's = 4 T's of Th's
- 8 H's of Th's - 3 H's of Th's = 5 H's of Th's

925,631
- 378,947
546,684

Do the following subtractions:

a.	b.	c.	d.
761,234	897,064	605,397	700,000
- 526,789	- 321,789	- 16,488	- 164,897
234,445	575,275	588,909	535,103

EXERCISES

Add:

a.	b.	c.	d.
213,416	89,253	55,758	254,312
651,251	37,625	79,801	73,175
20,002	18,749	194,311	2,267
+ 10,010	+ 27,942	84,070	197,038
894,679	**173,569**	+ 52,050	+ 43,208
		465,990	**570,000**

Subtract:

a.	b.	c.	d.
976,382	865,437	189,413	345,373
- 243,361	- 182,356	- 72,167	- 167,985
733,021	**683,081**	**117,246**	**177,388**

e.	f.	g.	h.
300,058	700,009	400,000	800,000
- 18,729	- 364,265	- 213,805	- 296,712
281,329	**335,744**	**186,195**	**503,288**

APPLICATIONS

1. In a city there are 347,879 males, and 319,658 females.
   a. How many people live in the city? <u>667,537</u>
   b. How many males are there more than females? <u>28,221</u>

2. The profits made by a company in three consecutive years were as follows:
   1st year: $395,276
   2nd year: $209,195
   3rd year: $190,486
   a. Find the total profits made in the three years. <u>$794,957</u>
   b. Find the difference between the highest and the lowest profits. <u>$204,790</u>

3. A + 71,284 = 94,867
   What number is A? <u>A = 23,583</u>

4. The sum of A, B, and C is 900,000.
   Given that A = 325,164 and B = 246,851, what number is C?
   <u>a. A + B = 572,015</u>
   <u>b. C = 327,985</u>

C

18 MULTIPLYING

Do the following multiplications:

a. $10 \times 29 =$ __290__
   $29 \times 10 =$ __290__

b. $100 \times 23 =$ __2,300__
   $23 \times 100 =$ __2,300__

You use the same principle to multiply larger numbers by 10, 100, 1000, … etc.
Do the following examples:

a. $1000 \times 29 =$ __29,000__
   $29 \times 1000 =$ __29,000__

b. $1000 \times 759 =$ __759,000__
   $759 \times 1000 =$ __759,000__

c. $100 \times 2,438 =$ __243,800__
   $2,438 \times 100 =$ __243,800__

d. $10 \times 4,386 =$ __43,860__
   $4,386 \times 10 =$ __43,860__

e. $1,000 \times 2,469 =$ __2,469,000__
   $2,469 \times 1,000 =$ __2,469,000__

f. $1,000 \times 3,470 =$ __3,470,000__
   $3,470 \times 1,000 =$ __3,470,000__

EXERCISE

Multiply:

1. a. $100 \times 34 =$ __3,400__
   c. $10 \times 4,350 =$ __43,500__
   e. $100 \times 346 =$ __34,600__
   g. $1,000 \times 149 =$ __149,000__
   i. $10 \times 37,569 =$ __375,000__
   k. $1,000 \times 240 =$ __240,000__
   m. $100 \times 3,100 =$ __310,000__
   o. $1,000 \times 260 =$ __260,000__

   b. $100 \times 79 =$ __7,900__
   d. $1,000 \times 67 =$ __67,000__
   f. $100 \times 2,768 =$ __276,800__
   h. $10 \times 45,896 =$ __458,960__
   j. $100 \times 3,469 =$ __346,900__
   l. $100 \times 280 =$ __28,000__
   n. $10 \times 5,4000 =$ __54,000__
   p. $100 \times 4,200 =$ __420,000__

2. a. $25 \times 100 =$ __2,500__
   c. $5,409 \times 10 =$ __54,090__
   e. $408 \times 100 =$ __40,800__
   g. $253 \times 1,000 =$ __253,000__
   i. $49,080 \times 10 =$ __490,800__
   k. $320 \times 1,000 =$ __320,000__
   m. $5,100 \times 100 =$ __510,000__
   o. $360 \times 1,000 =$ __360,000__

   b. $56 \times 100 =$ __5,600__
   d. $68 \times 1,000 =$ __68,000__
   f. $4,306 \times 100 =$ __430,600__
   h. $39,007 \times 10 =$ __390,070__
   j. $1,097 \times 100 =$ __109,700__
   l. $420 \times 100 =$ __42,000__
   n. $4,700 \times 10 =$ __47,000__
   p. $7,900 \times 100 =$ __790,000__

MULTIPLYING BY TENS, HUNDREDS, OR THOUSANDS

Do the following multiplications:

a. 20 x 40 = __800__ 20 x 46 = __920__	b. 30 x 80 = __2,400__ 30 x 87 = __2,610__
c. 40 x 200 = __8,000__ 40 x 235 = __9,400__	d. 200 x 40 = __8,000__ 200 x 48 = __9,600__

You use the same principle to multiply larger numbers by 10, 100, 1000, … etc. Do the following examples.

a. 30 x 400 = __12,000__ 30 x 427 = __12,810__	b. 90 x 700 = __63,000__ 90 x 706 = __63,540__
c. 300 x 80 = __24,000__ 300 x 89 = __26,700__	d. 700 x 60 = __42,000__ 700 x 69 = __48,300__
e. 800 x 900 = __720,000__ 800 x 970 = __776,000__	f. 500 x 800 = __400,000__ 500 x 801 = __400,500__
g. 500 x 830 = __415,000__ 500 x 831 = __415,500__	h. 800 x 960 = __768,000__ 800 x 976 = __780,800__

EXERCISES

Multiply:

1.	a. 40 x 700	= __28,000__	b. 900 x 50	= __45,000__
	c. 600 x 800	= __480,000__	d. 7,000 x 30	= __210,000__
	e. 80 x 500	= __40,000__	f. 90 x 800	= __72,000__
	g. 200 x 3,000	= __600,000__	h. 400 x 500	= __200,000__
	i. 70 x 9,000	= __630,000__	j. 6,000 x 90	= __540,000__
	k. 500 x 800	= __400,000__	l. 60 x 5,000	= __300,000__

2.	a. 30 x 280	= __8,400__	b. 70 x 370	= __25,900__
	c. 900 x 307	= __276,300__	d. 300 x 276	= __82,800__
	e. 90 x 4,368	= __393,120__	f. 50 x 3,006	= __150,300__
	g. 60 x 6,008	= __360,480__	h. 300 x 2,970	= __891,000__
	i. 80 x 4,505	= __360,400__	j. 40 x 5,050	= __202,000__
	k. 900 x 1,008	= __907,200__	l. 200 x 3,980	= __796,000__

Level 12

MULTIPLYING BY A ONE-DIGIT NUMERAL

- You know how to multiply a four-digit numeral by a one-digit numeral.
  Do the following examples:

a. 8 x 1,235 = 9,880	d. 2,536	e. 1,009	f. 1,125
b. 4 x 2,016 = 8,064	x 3	x 9	x 8
c. 6 x 1,505 = 9,030	7,608	9,081	9,000

- You can use the same principles in multiplying a 5-digit, 6-digit, or any other numeral by a one-digit numeral.
  You may use boxes:

THOUSANDS			ONES		
100'S	10'S	1'S	100'S	10'S	1'S
8	3	7	4	3	2

4 x 209,358 = $\boxed{8\ 3\ 7\ 4\ 3\ 2}$ = 837,432

Or you may do without the boxes:

a. 3 x 29,364 = 88,092	d. 78,345	e. 246,015	f. 19,005
b. 4 x 78,205 = 312,820	x 8	x 4	x 5
c. 9 x 107,308 = 965,772	626,760	984,060	95,025

EXERCISES

Multiply:

1.

a. 3 x 72,546 = 217,638	b. 5 x 23,873 = 119,365
c. 2 x 50,568 = 101,136	d. 7 x 25,652 = 179,564
e. 6 x 76,278 = 457,668	f. 9 x 98,724 = 888,516
g. 8 x 40,009 = 320,072	h. 6 x 50,034 = 300,204
i. 9 x 30,001 = 270,009	j. 5 x 80,004 = 400,020

2.

a. 3 x 213,123 = 639,369	b. 2 x 124,341 = 248,682
c. 7 x 124,315 = 870,205	d. 4 x 215,327 = 861,308
e. 4 x 200,305 = 801,220	f. 9 x 100,002 = 900,018
g. 6 x 150,035 = 900,210	h. 5 x 108,036 = 540,180
i. 7 x 101,204 = 708,428	j. 3 x 200,307 = 600,921

3.

a. 67,384 x 5 = 336,920	b. 90,306 x 7 = 632,142	c. 30,002 x 4 = 120,008	d. 90,106 x 8 = 720,848

4.

a. 125,328 x 7 = 877,296	b. 309,205 x 3 = 927,615	c. 200,005 x 4 = 800,020	d. 107,604 x 8 = 860,832

MULTIPLYING BY A TWO OR THREE-DIGIT NUMERAL

Example 1.
You want to multiply: 35 x 489

Discussion:
You multiply step by step:
a. 5 x 489 = 2445
b. 30 x 489 = 14670
c. add: 17115

```
  489        489
x  35      x  35
 2445   or  2445
14670       1467
17115       17115
```

Example 2.
You want to multiply: 235 x 489

Discussion:
You want to multiply step by step.
a. 5 x 489 = 2445
b. 30 x 489 = 14670
c. 200 x 489 = 97800
d. add: 114,915

```
   489         489
 x 235       x 235
  2445   or   2445
 14670        1467
 97800         987
114,915      114,915
```

Example 3.
You want to multiply 308 x 697

Discussion:
You multiply step by step.
a. 8 x 697 = 5576
b. 300 x 697 = 209100
c. add: 214676

```
   697         679
 x 308       x 308
  5576   or   5576
209100        2091
214676       214676
```

Do the following multiplications:

a. 158	b. 296	c. 317	d. 819
x 39	x 57	x 56	x 25
1422	2072	1902	4095
474	1480	1585	1638
6162	16872	17752	20475

e. 1368	f. 7259	g. 4328	h. 8604
x 23	x 47	x 26	x 36
4104	50813	25968	51624
2736	29036	8656	25812
31464	341173	112528	309744

EXERCISES

Multiply:

a.　　694 x 118 5552 694 694 81892	b.　　325 x 183 975 2600 325 59475	c.　　379 x 215 1895 379 758 81485	d.　　294 x 386 1764 2352 882 113484
e.　　1289 x 237 9023 3867 2578 305493	f.　　1108 x 376 6648 7756 3324 416608	g.　　2949 x 268 23592 17694 5898 790332	h.　　1680 x 397 11760 15120 5040 666960
i.　　2304 x 298 18432 20736 4608 686592	j.　　5120 x 145 25600 20480 5120 742400	k.　　6170 x 112 12340 6170 6170 691040	l.　　3105 x 317 21735 3105 9315 984285
m.　　365 x 270 2555 730 98550	n.　　656 x 380 5248 1968 249280	o.　　540 x 230 1620 1080 124200	p.　　705 x 310 705 2115 218550
q.　　1250 x 105 6250 1250 131250	r.　　307 x 206 1842 614 63242	s.　　225 x 107 1575 225 24075	t.　　3702 x 205 18510 7404 758910

APPLICATIONS

1. A builder built 8 houses for the
   total cost of $600,000.
   He sold the houses for $95,900 each.
   How much profit did he make?

   a. 8 x $95,900 = $767,200
   b. $767,200 - $600,000 = $167,200

2. A theater which has 1,575 seats was full
   for 25 consecutive shows.
   a. How many persons attended the shows?
   b. If the ticket cost $8, how much money
      was collected in all three shows?

   a. 25 x 1,575 = 39,375
   b. 39,375 x $8 = $315,000

3. A newspaper sells 125,125 copies daily
   during the week (Monday - Saturday), and
   238,395 copies on Sunday.
   How many copies are sold all week?

   a. 6 x 125,125 = 750,750
   b. 750,750 + 238,395 = 989,145

4. A = 30 x 298 and B = 70 x 650
   Find the sum of A and B.
   Find the difference between A and B.

   a. A = 8,940 and B = 45,500
   b. A + B = 54,440
   c. B - A = 36,560

5. Find the answer:

a. 70,000 - (305 x 208)	b. (402 x 306) - 97,258
70,000 - 63,440 = 6,560	123,012 - 97,258 = 25,754
c. (39 x 415) + (68 x 229)	d. (109 x 306) - (95 x 207)
16,185 + 15,572 = 31,757	33,354 - 19,665 = 13,689

DIVIDING

Do the following divisions:

a.	b.	c.
$\dfrac{0921}{4)\ 3684}$	$\dfrac{1357}{5)\ 6785}$	$\dfrac{0908}{9)\ 8176}\,\text{R4}$

• You use the same procedure in dividing a 5-place, 6-place, or any other numeral by one-digit numeral.

Do the following divisions:

a.	b.	c.
$\dfrac{21992}{4)\ 87968}$	$\dfrac{1071}{6)\ 6426}$	$\dfrac{06790}{8)\ 54324}\,\text{R4}$
d.	e.	f.
$\dfrac{076088}{9)\ 684792}$	$\dfrac{134705}{7)\ 942935}$	$\dfrac{106090}{8)\ 848725}\,\text{R5}$

EXERCISES

Divide:

a.	b.	c.
$\dfrac{312123}{3)\ 936369}$	$\dfrac{241132}{2)\ 482264}$	$\dfrac{211121}{4)\ 844484}$
d.	e.	f.
$\dfrac{192651}{5)\ 963255}$	$\dfrac{291418}{3)\ 874254}$	$\dfrac{050879}{6)\ 305274}$
g.	h.	i.
$\dfrac{035066}{7)\ 245468}\,\text{R6}$	$\dfrac{192974}{5)\ 964872}\,\text{R2}$	$\dfrac{050132}{6)\ 300795}\,\text{R3}$
j.	k.	l.
$\dfrac{24047}{2)\ 48094}$	$\dfrac{279024}{3)\ 837072}$	$\dfrac{065015}{5)\ 325075}$
m.	n.	o.
$\dfrac{120132}{7)\ 840924}$	$\dfrac{160118}{6)\ 960708}$	$\dfrac{120119}{8)\ 960952}$
p.	q.	r.
$\dfrac{125009}{6)\ 750058}\,\text{R4}$	$\dfrac{065004}{8)\ 520036}\,\text{R4}$	$\dfrac{085002}{4)\ 340009}\,\text{R1}$

C

Do the following divisions:

a.	b.	c.
0036 $48)\overline{1728}$ $\underline{144}$ 288 $\underline{288}$	0120 $75)\overline{9000}$ $\underline{75}$ 150 $\underline{150}$	0302 $25)\overline{7550}$ $\underline{75}$ 50 $\underline{50}$

You follow the same procedure in dividing a 5-place, 6-place, or any number by another number.

Do the following divisions:

a.	b.	c.
00920 $25)\overline{23000}$ 225 50 $\underline{50}$	00306 $85)\overline{26010}$ $\underline{255}$ 510 $\underline{510}$	003060 $128)\overline{391680}$ $\underline{384}$ 768 $\underline{768}$

EXCERCISES

Divide:

a.	b.	c.
00438 $52)\overline{22776}$ $\underline{208}$ 197 $\underline{156}$ 416 $\underline{416}$	00552 $87)\overline{48024}$ $\underline{435}$ 452 $\underline{435}$ 174 $\underline{174}$	00679 $93)\overline{63147}$ $\underline{558}$ 734 $\underline{651}$ 837 $\underline{837}$
d.	e.	f.
005986 $34)\overline{203524}$ $\underline{170}$ 335 $\underline{306}$ 292 $\underline{272}$ 204 $\underline{204}$	003148 $58)\overline{182584}$ $\underline{174}$ 85 $\underline{58}$ 278 $\underline{232}$ 464 $\underline{464}$	007384 $79)\overline{583336}$ $\underline{553}$ 303 $\underline{237}$ 663 $\underline{632}$ 316 $\underline{316}$

EXERCISES

Divide:

a. $\quad$ 00135 125)16875 $\underline{125}$ 437 $\underline{375}$ 625 $\underline{625}$	b. $\quad$ 00348 245)85260 $\underline{735}$ 1176 $\underline{980}$ 1960 $\underline{1960}$	c. $\quad$ 000425 397)168725 $\underline{1588}$ 992 $\underline{794}$ 1985 $\underline{1985}$
d. $\quad$ 00026 385)10010 $\underline{770}$ 2310 $\underline{2310}$	e. $\quad$ 000318 1215)386370 $\underline{3645}$ 2187 $\underline{1215}$ 9720 $\underline{9720}$	f. $\quad$ 000356 1173)417588 $\underline{3519}$ 6568 $\underline{5865}$ 7038 $\underline{7038}$
g. $\quad$ 00350 65)22750 $\underline{195}$ 325 $\underline{325}$	h. $\quad$ 01700 42)71400 $\underline{42}$ 294 $\underline{294}$	i. $\quad$ 00280 138)38640 $\underline{276}$ 1104 $\underline{1104}$
j. $\quad$ 00708 36)25488 $\underline{252}$ 288 $\underline{288}$	k. $\quad$ 00509 72)36648 $\underline{360}$ 648 $\underline{648}$	l. $\quad$ 00105 485)50925 $\underline{485}$ 2425 $\underline{2425}$
m. $\quad$ 01020 42)42840 $\underline{42}$ 84 $\underline{84}$	n. $\quad$ 02003 36)72108 $\underline{72}$ 108 $\underline{108}$	o. $\quad$ 001006 127)127762 $\underline{127}$ 762 $\underline{762}$

C

1. a. What number do you subtract
        from 38216 for the answer to
        be divisible by 125?   91

$$\begin{array}{r} 00305 \\ 125\overline{)38216} \\ 375 \\ \hline 716 \\ 625 \\ \hline 91 \\ 91 \\ \hline \end{array}$$

    b. What number do you add to
        38216 for the answer to be
        divisible by 125?   34

2. a. In the division to the right,   01290
        what is the missing number?   56)   56 x 1290 = 72240

    b. In the division to the right,   009021
        what is the missing number?   )676575   676575 ÷ 9021 = 75

3. A = (50225 ÷ 245) + 2738
    What number is A?

    a. 50225 ÷ 245 = 205
    b. 205 + 2738 = 2943

4. 24 x N = 13920
    What number is N?

    N = 13920 ÷ 24 = 580

5. You multiplied a number by 39 and then
    added 848. The answer was 23,000.
    What was the number?

    a. 23,000 - 848 = 22152
    b. 22,152 ÷ 39 = 568

6. (2 x A) + 3400 = 5800
    What number is A?

    a. 2 x A = 5800 - 3400 = 2400
    b. A = 2400 ÷ 2 = 1200

- 1,000 thousands is a million. It is written 1,000,000.
  In millions, you can count up to 999 million.
  You can write a 9-place numeral, such as the one shown below:

MILLIONS			THOUSANDS			ONES		
100'S	10'S	1'S	100'S	10'S	1'S	100'S	10'S	1'S
9	3	6	2	7	8	1	4	5

= 936,278,145

- 1,000 millions is a billion. It is written 1,000,000,000.
  In billions, you can count up to 999 billions.
  You can write a 12-place numeral such as the one shown below:

BILLIONS			MILLIONS			THOUSANDS			ONES		
100'S	10'S	1'S	100'S	10'S	1'S	100'S	10'S	1'S	100'S	10'S	1'S
1	9	4	2	0	6	3	7	8	5	0	0

= 194,206,378,500

- 1,000 billions make 1 trillion. It is written 1,000,000,000,000.
  In trillions, you can count up to 999 trillions.
  You can write a 15-place numeral, such as the one shown below:

TRILLIONS			BILLIONS			MILLIONS			THOUSANDS			ONES		
100'S	10'S	1'S	100'S	10'S	1'S	100'S	10'S	1'S	100'S	10'S	1'S	100'S	10'S	1'S
3	8	7	4	9	6	2	7	1	5	6	9	3	2	8

= 387,496,271,569,328

- In any numeral, from the right to left:
a. The first 3 digits stand for ones.
   They are called the ones period.
b. The second 3 digits stand for thousands.
   They are called the thousands period.
c. The third 3 digits stand for millions.
   They are called the millions period.
d. The fourth 3 digits stand for billions.
   They are called the billions period.
e. The fifth 3 digits stand for trillions.
   They are called the trillions period.

564,489,207,138,607

- Using the number periods, you can read and write any numeral:
a. 5,000,007 is read "five million seven."
b. 185,000,097 is read, "one hundred eighty-five million ninety-seven."
c. 28,785,439,370 is read, "twenty-eight billion seven hundred eighty-five million four hundred thirty-nine thousand three hundred seventy."
d. Three million seven hundred eighty thousand five hundred ninety is written 3,780,509.
e. Seventeen billion eight million ninety thousand twenty-four is written 17,008,090,024.

APPLICATIONS

1. In the numeral to the right: **270,084,650,100,903**
   a. What does 6 represent?   6 H's of millions
   b. What does 4 represent?   4 billions
   c. What does 7 represent?   7 T's of trillions
   d. What does 1 represent?   1 H of thousands
   e. What does 8 represent?   8 T's of billions
   f. What does 2 represent?   2 H's of trillions

2. a. Write the number which is 275 thousand more than 5 million.   5,275,000
   b. Write the number which is 3 hundred more than 7 million.   7,000,300
   c. Write the number which is 6 million more than 8 billion.   8,006,000,000
   d. Write the number which is 29 more than 17 million.   17,000,029
   e. Write the number which is 127 more than 4 trillion.   4,000,000,000,127

3. a. Write the number which is read "nine million seventeen thousand."   9,017,000
   b. Write the number which is read, "six billion nine thousand."   6,000,009,000
   c. Write the number which is read, "Four trillion twenty six."   4,000,000,000,026
   d. Write the number which is read, "Ninety trillion, three billion."   90,003,000,000,000

4. a. How many thousands are in 5 millions?   5,000
   b. How many millions are in 8 billions?   8,000
   c. How many billions are in 7 trillions?   7,000
   d. How many thousands are in 1 billion?   1,000,000
   e. How many millions are in 1 trillion?   1,000,000

5. a. How many millions are in 6,000 thousands?   6
   b. How many billions are in 9,000 millions?   9
   c. How many trillions are in 7,000 billions?   7

EXERCISES

In adding, subtracting, multiplying, and dividing large numbers, you follow the same procedures you have followed before. You only have to be careful in placing the digits in their appropriate places.

1. Add:

a.		b.		c.	
	924,395,864		9,736,207		3,518,398,724
	271,480,698		1,600,914		9,614,804,207
	721,364,872		2,787,227		8,907,008,493
	+ 694,279,488		+ 5,509,352		+ 14,258,679,999
	2,611,520,922		19,633,700		36,298,891,423

2. Subtract:

a.		b.		c.	
	23,764,271		25,300,948		14,000,000
	- 9,864,936		- 9,484,672		- 3,708,694
	13,899,335		15,816,276		10,291,306
d.		e.		f.	
	314,268,007		279,416,000		310,000,000
	- 98,279,948		- 68,172,904		- 71,604,702
	215,988,059		211,243,096		238,395,298

3. Multiply:

a.		b.		c.	
	9,429,376		34,279,588		2,397,648,789
	x 8		x 5		x 8
	75,435,008		171,397,940		19,181,190,312

d.		e.		f.	
	9,748		17,978		13,908
	x 269		x 3,006		x 4,605
	87732		107868		69540
	58488		53934		83448
	19496		54,041,868		55632
	2,622,212				64,046,340

4. Divide:

a.		b.		c.	
	07,789,569		082,663,045		0,391,352,656
	5) 38,947,845		9) 743,967,405		7) 2,739,468,592
d.		e.		f.	
	197,617,050		061,209,255		120,018,051
	4) 790,468,200		8) 489,674,040		6) 720,108,306

APPLICATIONS

1. From 1970 to 1980, the population of the United States of America increased from 203,235,000 to 226,546,000. How much was the increase?

   $$\begin{array}{r} 226,546,000 \\ -\ 203,235,000 \\ \hline 23,311,000 \end{array}$$

2. According to the 1980 census, the three most popular states were:

   California 23,667,900
   New York 17,558,100
   Texas 14,229,200

   a. How many more people lived in California than in New York? 6,109,800
   b. How many fewer people lived Texas than in New York? 3,328,900

3. Long Island (New York) is composed of two counties: Nassau and Suffolk. The table to the right gives the population of the two counties in 1970 and 1980.

	1970	1980
Nassau	1,428,838	1,321,600
Suffolk	1,127,030	1,284,200

   a. In 1970, how many people lived on Long Island? 2,555,868
   b. In 1980, how many people lived on Long Island? 2,605,800
   c. What was the increase from 1970 to 1980? 49,932

4. The difference between two numbers is 29,384,600.

a. If the smaller number is 15,183,968, what is the other number?	b. If the larger number is 40,000,200, what is the other number?
$\begin{array}{r} 29,384,600 \\ +\ 15,183,968 \\ \hline 44,568,568 \end{array}$	$\begin{array}{r} 40,000,200 \\ -\ 29,384,600 \\ \hline 10,615,600 \end{array}$

5. A is 3,967,426 less than B.

a. If A is 2,784,271, what number is B? $\begin{array}{r} 3,967,426 \\ +\ 2,784,271 \\ \hline 6,751,697 \end{array}$	b. If B is 5,405,207, what number is A? $\begin{array}{r} 5,405,207 \\ -\ 3,967,426 \\ \hline 1,437,781 \end{array}$

6. M is 5 times N.

a. If N is 8,648,435, what number is M? $\begin{array}{r} 8,648,435 \\ \times\ \ \ \ \ \ \ 5 \\ \hline 43,242,175 \end{array}$	b. If M is 8,648,435. what number is N? $\begin{array}{r} 1,729,687 \\ \hline 5)\,8,648,435 \end{array}$

C

Level 12

UNIT C TEST

1. a. Use the digits 5, 3, 2, 9, 0, 8.
   to form the largest number you can. _____985,320_____
   b. Use the digits 5, 3, 2, 9, 0, 8
   to form the smallest number you can. _____023,589_____

2. a. In the numeral 321,425 what does 1 stand for? _____1 thousand_____
   b. In the numeral 321,425 what does 3 stand for? _____3 H's of Th's_____

3. a. How many T's of Th's are in 3H's of Th's ? _____30_____
   b. How many T's of Th's are in 60 Th's? _____6_____
   c. How would you group 94 Th's? _____9 T's of Th and 4 Th's_____

4. Add:

a. 234,102	b. 136,129	c. 123,766	d. 251,938
101,341	213,937	98,838	51,791
42,013	89,853	76,199	272,787
+ 321,321	67,086	120,484	103,470
698,777	+ 109,795	+ 53,252	+ 60,014
	616,800	**472,539**	**740,000**

5. Subtract:

a. 987,645	b. 837,612	c. 380,726	d. 700,000
- 264,231	- 18,729	- 99,213	- 271,842
723,414	**818,883**	**281,513**	**428,158**

6. A is a number. You subtracted
   85,729 and then added 98,401.
   The answer was 300,000.   a. $300,000 - 98,401 = 201,599$
   What was the number?   b. $201,599 + 85,729 = 287,328$

7. Subtract the sum of 398,271 and   a. $398,271 + 179,306 = 577,577$
   179,306 from 800,000.   b. $800,000 - 577,577 = 222,423$

8. $N - 379,668 = 209,467$
   What number is N? $N = 209,467 + 379,668 = 589,135$

9. Multiply:
   a. 2 x 243,412 = __486,824__
   b. 6 x 38,432 = __230,592__
   c. 3 x 68,273 = __204,819__
   d. 8 x 86,325 = __690,600__

10. Multiply:
    a. 100 x 100 = __10,000__
    b. 100 x 1,000 = __100,000__
    c. 50 x 400 = __20,000__
    d. 700 x 60 = __42,000__
    e. 600 x 600 = __360,000__
    f. 80 x 3,000 = __240,000__

11. Multiply:
    a. 90 x 378 = __34,020__
    b. 3000 x 29 = __87,000__
    c. 316 x 200 = __63,200__
    d. 314 x 500 = __157,000__
    e. 78 x 5000 = __390,000__
    f. 1230 x 400 = __492,000__

12. Multiply:

a.	b.	c.
972 x 48 7776 3888 46656	804 x 25 4020 1608 20100	950 x 38 7600 2850 36100
d.	e.	f.
675 x 328 5400 1350 2025 221400	256 x 490 2304 1024 125440	723 x 105 3615 72300 75915

13. Divide:

a.	b.	c.
__421,342__ 2) 842,684	__210,031__ 3) 630,093	__151,967__ 5) 759,835
d.	e.	f.
__032,298__ 8) 258,384	__130,893__ 6) 785,358	__090,031__ 4) 360,124

14. Divide:

a.	b.	c.
__00461__ 29) 13369 116 176 174 29 29	__00105__ 549) 57645 549 2745 2745	__00390__ 235) 91650 705 2115 2115

C

15. On weekdays a newspaper sells
    93,728 copies daily. On Sunday
    it sells 34,625 copies more.
    How many copies are sold in one week?

    a. 6 x 93,728 = 562,368
    b. 93,728 + 34,625 = 128,353
    c. 562,368 + 128,353 = 690,721

16. a. You have 39,168 items. You want to
       divide them into sets, 128 items each.
       What is the result?   306 sets are made.
    b. You have 39,168 items. You want to
       divide them equally into 128 sets.
       What is the result?   306 items in each set.

$$\begin{array}{r} 00306 \\ 128\overline{)39168} \\ 384 \\ \hline 768 \\ 768 \end{array}$$

17. A builder spent $600,000 on 6 identical
    houses. He paid $147,750 for the land
    and the rest was spent on construction.
    How much was spent on the construction
    of each house?

    a. $600,000 - $147,750 = $452,250
    b. $452,250 ÷ 6 = $75,375

18. The sum of two numbers is 235,000.
    One of the numbers is 95,658.
    What is the other number?

    235,000 - 95,658 = 139,342

19. 7 x a number is 468,314.
    What is the number?

    468,314 ÷ 7 = 66,902

20. N = 325 x 218
    M = N - 25000
    What number is M?

    a. N = 70,850
    b. M = 70,850 - 25,000 = 45,850

21. a. What is a million?   1,000 thousands
    b. What is a billion?   1,000 millions
    c. What is a trillion?   1,000 billions

22. The letters to the right stand for digits in a numeral.   YMH,CAD,BXM,GNF,TVS
    a. What does N stand for?   tens of thousands
    b. What does X stand for?   tens of millions
    c. What does Y stand for?   hundreds of trillions

23. Write the numeral which is read:
    a. Seven million six thousand   7,006,000
    b. Twenty-eight billion three million   28,003,000,000
    c. Nine billion thirty-five   9,000,000,035
    d. Eight billion six million four   8,006,000,004

24. a. Write the number which is 35 million
       more than 7 billion.   7,035,000,000
    b. Write the number which is 85 more
       than 6 million.   6,000,085
    c. Write the number which is 80 thousand
       more than 26 million.   26,080,000

---

25. Add:

a.		b.		c.	
	379,268,494		7,480,618		360,789,248
	39,607,320		2,976,314		438,216,843
+	48,268,481	+	4,097,026	+	273,625,909
	467,144,295		14,553,958		1,072,632,000

---

26. Subtract:

a.		b.		c.	
	39,648,271		87,263,000		90,000,000
-	9,423,784	-	48,372,976	-	48,304,206
	30,224,487		38,890,024		41,695,794

---

27. Multiply:

a.		b.		c.	
	15,706		3,504		12,107
x	2,009	x	924	x	3,201
	141,354		14,016		12,107
	31,412,000		70,080		2,421,400
	31,553,354		3,153,600		36,321,000
			3,237,696		38,754,507

---

28. Divide:

a.		b.		c.	
	04,234,375		11,682,168		027,090,306
	8) 33,875,000		6) 70,093,008		5) 135,451,530

---

29. The population of a state changed
    from 2,678,287 to 3,107,569.   3,107,569 - 2,678,287 = 429,282
    What was the change?   An increase of 429,282 people

30. What number do you multiply by 8 for
    the product to be 300,832,416?   300,832,416 ÷ 8 = 37,604,052

Level 12

31. Using only the digits to the right: 2, 5, 9, 4, 3, 1, 0

     a. What is the largest number you can write?   <u>9,543,210</u>

     b. What is the smallest number you can write?   <u>123,459</u>

     c. What is the sum of the the two numbers?   <u>9,666,669</u>

     d. What is the difference between the two numbers?   <u>9,419,751</u>

---

32. A, B, and C are three numbers. A is 9,673,109 and B is 2,683,298. A + B + C is 15,000,000. What number is C?

     <u>2,643,593</u>

     C = 15,000,000 - (A + B)
       = 15,000,000 - (9,673,109 + 2,683,298)
       = 15,000,000 - 12,356,407

---

33. The sum of two numbers 90,000. One number is 10,000 greater than the other?

     a. What is the smaller number?   <u>40,000</u>

     $\frac{1}{2}$ x (90,000 - 10,000)

     $\frac{1}{2}$ x 80,000

     b. What is the larger number?   <u>50,000</u>
     40,000 + 10,000